Simply 7

Simply 7

Quick Southwest Recipes
Just 7 Ingredients Away

by Kelley Cleary Coffeen

photography by Christopher Marchetti

 Northland Publishing

www.northlandpub.com

Composed in the United States of America
Printed in Hong Kong

Edited by Tammy Gales
Designed by Katie Jennings
Production supervised by Donna Boyd

We would like to offer a special "thank you" to Aunt Maude at
Aunt Maude's Antique Mall, Jerean and Tom Hutchinson at La Posta de Mesilla,
and Sally and Hal Jones at Jones & Co. Jewelers for letting us photograph
their beautiful antique clocks and Southwest accessories.

The use of trade names does not imply an endorsement by the product manufacturer.

FIRST IMPRESSION 2003
ISBN 0-87358-842-8

03   04   05   06   07   5   4   3   2   1

Library of Congress Cataloging-in-Publication Data
Coffeen, Kelley.
Simply 7 : quick Southwest recipes just seven ingredients away / by Kelley Cleary Coffeen.
p. cm.
1. Cookery, American—Southwestern style. 2. Quick and easy cookery.
I. Title: Simply seven. II. Title.
TX715.2.S69C645 2003   641.5'55—dc21
2003053973

I dedicate this book

to my loving parents, Frances and Edward J. Cleary,

who showered me with love and encouragement

and gave me strength, enabling me to enjoy and persevere

through the many seasons of life.

—KCC

Contents

INTRODUCTION **1**

TIME-SAVING TIPS **3**

SOUTHWEST STARTERS **5**

SAVORY SOUPS & SALADS **21**

MAIN MEALS **37**

    RISE & SHINE

    LIGHT BITES

    ENTRÉES

SIMPLE SIDES **73**

SWEETS OF THE SOUTHWEST **83**

LIVELY LIBATIONS **97**

SEASONAL SELECTIONS **106**

INDEX **108**

ACKNOWLEDGEMENTS **111**

On any given day of the week I find myself picking kids up, dropping kids off, weaving doctors appointments and parent-teacher conferences in between marketing and business meetings, and juggling my responsibilities. Some days I think I've got it, and there are others when I know I am over committed. So cooking a few meals for the family during the week can be overwhelming at best. It used to be that my kids begged to go out for fast food. These days I find myself apologizing for eating too many fast food dinners in one week! That's why I know how America wants to cook. I live it every day. When I cook, it has to be quick, easy, and bursting with flavor.

That's how I cook on television. That's right! Every week in El Paso, Texas I have the opportunity to share flavorful recipes with my television audience in West Texas and Southern New Mexico. Since the show began airing in 1998, I've developed what I call a "7/30 cooking concept" for "Kelley's Kitchen." My recipes contain no more than 7 ingredients, and I try to keep the actual hands-on preparation time to 30 minutes, excluding baking or roasting time.

My viewers have become loyal fans of "Kelley's Kitchen." They like how I combine high-quality prepared foods with fresh ingredients. This not only shortens the process, but also allows me to keep the ingredient list to a minimum. And of course, each recipe is laced with the wonderfully rich flavors of the Southwest. I infuse the fresh produce and herbs of this region with the unique cooking techniques of our neighbors south of the border to bring together an array of southwestern-style cuisine that is simple and tasty.

Start your day with fluffy Pumpkin Pancakes or a chile-style Fiesta Breakfast full of Southwest flavors. Simple starters like my Sassy Shrimp Salsa or Sweet Hot Cheese Spread keep entertaining fun and festive. Explore the fresh, fiery flavors of my Chile Corn Chowder and Latino Salsa Salad. You'll also want to try my enticing entrées like Sour Cream Chicken Enchiladas, Pastrami and Pepper Jack Wraps, or Marinated Pork Loin Chops with Mango Salsa, all tantalizing and delicious but simple to prepare.

My Channel 9 viewers also like the seasonal approach I use on "Kelley's Kitchen." There is quite a bit of diversity in our culinary cravings throughout the year, and I believe that those cravings are directly related to the four seasons. The majority of people crave different types of foods as the weather changes—hearty chowders and stews during the Autumn months, while rich, roasted meats make tempting entrées for a winter holiday dinner. Spring brings the yearning to eat lighter and healthier, and of course, summer means entertaining outdoors, requiring fresh, fun fare. If you are interested in satisfying your culinary cravings, pay attention to the seasonal icons offered on each page, or, for a more detailed selection, you will find a complete seasonal menu listing on pages 106-107. No matter what season you are cooking for, take a walk through my culinary calendar, and you will find just the right recipe.

So, keeping these three elements in mind—simple, Southwest, and seasonal— I have gathered my best recipes and offer them to you in this cookbook. *Simply 7: Quick Southwest Recipes Just Seven Ingredients Away* will take you through the year, giving you delicious ideas and quick recipes that are sure to become family favorites. You will like how I cook, because I cook the way America wants to cook—simple, easy, and stress free.

 SPRING

 SUMMER

 AUTUMN

 WINTER

Top 10 Time-saving Tips

1. I like to plan a weekly cooking strategy. I don't always stick to it, (kids activities usually take over by mid-week), but it does help keep me fairly organized. I plan to cook two full meals during the week, eat out one meal, plan one day for leftovers, and leave Friday open.

2. Read through each recipe you are about to prepare. Make sure you know and are familiar with each ingredient and you understand each step of the instructions.

3. Shop on Sunday or Monday so you can stay in control of the meal plan for the rest of the week.

4. Restock fresh produce and fruits with a quick mid-week grocery stop, especially in the spring and summer months when the produce is fresh.

5. Keep the pantry, freezer, and refrigerator organized so you know what you have on hand. Check all three areas before you make your shopping list.

6. Keep extra prepared soups, canned and frozen vegetables, and frozen meats and chicken on hand in order to whip up a quick savory soup or stew, especially in the winter months.

7. Keep high-quality prepared foods such as sauces, salsas, salad dressings, and condiments on hand in order to enhance or create tasty entrées and side dishes in a hurry.

8. Work ahead of your timeline. Prepare "do ahead" dishes a day earlier to reduce stress and clean up time before serving or entertaining.

9. Give each family member a job in the kitchen—setting the table, filling the glasses, making the salad, clearing the table. Get everyone working together.

10. When preparing a large meal with multiple recipes, clean up after each one. This reduces clutter in the kitchen and long hours of clean up after the meal.

Southwest Starters

Spicy appetizers, snacks, and salsas are the festive beginnings of any southwestern gathering. I like to offer an adventurous array of unusual flavors for my guests to experience, but I don't want to spend hours in the kitchen! I have collected and created some tried and true favorites that are easy on the host and a culinary delight for my friends and family. Choose from simple "toss together" recipes like Black Bean Basil Salsa or Sassy Shrimp Salsa, both of which are perfect for spur of the moment entertaining. Or, serve up a plate of Fresh Fruit and Sweet Creams, Spicy Stuffed Mushrooms with a little kick, and endless bowls of Baked Artichoke Queso. My philosophy is to keep it simple, keep it tasty, and keep it fun!

Southwest Snack Mix

Pico de Gallo

Fresh Salsa Verde

Apple-Onion-Garlic Salsa

Black Bean Basil Salsa

Mango Salsa

Sassy Shrimp Salsa

Chile-Spiced Pecans

Spicy Stuffed Mushrooms

Fresh Fruit and Sweet Creams

Garden Salsa Nachos

Nachos Rancheros

Pesto Tomato Bruschette

Pepper Garlic Cheese Bread

**Rosemary Garlic
    Focaccia Bread**

Sweet Hot Cheese Spread

Baked Artichoke Queso

2 cups Bugles corn chips

3 cups stick pretzels

2 cups Goldfish cheese crackers

2 cups peanuts

4 cups Crispix cereal

1 package (1 ¼ ounces) taco
seasoning mix

¾ cup vegetable oil

Southwest Snack Mix

*My kids love this snack mix. It's spicy, fun to eat, and a blast to make.
Shake it up for a crowd.*

Place the corn chips, pretzels, cheese crackers, peanuts, and
cereal in a brown paper bag. In a separate bowl, combine
the taco mix and oil. Mix well and drizzle over the cereal
mix in the bag. Close the bag and shake until the cereal mixture is well blended. 🦋 [Makes 6 to 8 Servings]

4 TO 6 VINE-RIPENED TOMATOES,
SEEDED AND CHOPPED

2 TO 3 JALAPEÑO CHILES, SEEDED
AND CHOPPED

2 SERRANO CHILES, SEEDED
AND CHOPPED

1 LARGE YELLOW ONION, CHOPPED

4 GREEN ONIONS, FINELY CHOPPED

2 TABLESPOONS FRESH CILANTRO,
CHOPPED

JUICE OF 2 LIMES

Pico de Gallo

Pico de Gallo literally means "Rooster's Beak." Some say the name comes from the similarity of the chopping sound of a cook's knife to the pecking sound of a rooster. No matter what the significance is, though, these flavors capture the true essence of Mexico. This salsa is muy picante, "very spicy!"

Gently combine the tomato, chiles, onions, and cilantro. Add the lime juice. Mix well and refrigerate, stirring occasionally. Refrigerate for at least 1 hour. Serve with corn tortilla chips. ❄ [Makes 4 to 6 servings]

12 TOMATILLOS, PEELED, CORED,
AND CHOPPED

1 TO 2 CLOVES GARLIC, PEELED

1 SMALL BUNCH CILANTRO, MINCED

6 GREEN ONIONS, CHOPPED

3 FRESH JALAPEÑO CHILES, SEEDED
AND CHOPPED

½ TEASPOON KOSHER SALT

1 RIPE AVOCADO, CUBED

Fresh Salsa Verde

I love this summer salsa. The raw tomatillos give it an almost citrusy bite, and it makes a fun dipping sauce for tacos and chips. Drop a spoonful in tortilla soup or frijoles, or drizzle it across your grilled fish fillets.

Place the tomatillos, garlic, cilantro, green onions, jalapeños, and salt in a blender or food processor and pulse until the onions are processed, about 10 to 15 seconds. Pulse a few more times if needed, but do not process until completely smooth. Pour into an airtight container, and chill for 1 to 2 hours to allow the flavors to blend. Before serving, add the avocado cubes. Serve with corn tortilla chips or over your favorite meal. ☀ [Makes 4 to 6 servings]

Apple-Onion-Garlic Salsa

This salsa goes especially well with pork or chicken dishes. Try it with my Pork Loin Fajitas (pg. 60) and liven up your dinner table!

Combine the oil and sugar in a large skillet over medium-high heat, stirring until the sugar is dissolved. Add garlic, onion, apple, and bell pepper. Cook for 2 minutes. Add the vinegar to the pan and deglaze, scraping the bottom of the pan to dislodge any browned bits. Blend well and serve with pork or chicken fajitas. ✳ [Makes 4 to 6 servings]

1 TABLESPOON VEGETABLE OIL

1 TABLESPOON SUGAR

3 MEDIUM CLOVES GARLIC, CHOPPED

1 LARGE WHITE ONION,
   CUT INTO STRIPS

2 GRANNY SMITH APPLES,
   COARSELY CHOPPED

1 LARGE RED BELL PEPPER, STEMMED,
   SEEDED, AND CUT INTO 1/4-INCH STRIPS

2 TABLESPOONS RICE VINEGAR

2 CANS (15 OUNCES EACH)
BLACK BEANS
⅓ CUP OLIVE OIL
3 TABLESPOONS BALSAMIC VINEGAR
½ CUP FRESH BASIL, CHOPPED
2 CLOVES GARLIC, MINCED
¼ TEASPOON RED PEPPER FLAKES
SALT AND PEPPER TO TASTE

3 MEDIUM-SIZED FRESH MANGOS,
PEELED, SEEDED, AND CUT INTO
¼-INCH CHUNKS (SEE NOTE)
1 MEDIUM RED ONION,
THINLY SLICED AND DICED
1 RED BELL PEPPER, DICED
2 FRESH JALAPEÑO PEPPERS,
SEEDED AND DICED

Black Bean Basil Salsa

Tangy balsamic vinegar and basil give this bean salsa a new dimension. It's a rich and filling appetizer that your guests won't soon forget.

Rinse and drain the beans, and place them in a large mixing bowl. Gently combine the olive oil, vinegar, basil, garlic, and red pepper flakes. Salt and pepper to taste. Let the salsa sit for at least 1 hour, tossing occasionally. Serve with corn tortilla chips. ☀ [Makes 6 to 8 servings]

Mango Salsa

The rich velvety texture of mangos combined with fresh chile and onions creates an adventurous salsa that really compliments roasted pork, chicken, or crispy corn tortilla chips.

In a medium-sized bowl, gently combine the mangos, red onion, red bell pepper, and fresh jalapeno. Chill until ready to serve.

Note: If mangos are out of season, substitute mangos in a jar, found near the produce section of your grocery store. ☀ [Makes 4 to 6 servings]

Sassy Shrimp Salsa

This combination of hot chile and fresh seafood gives a tantalizing twist to your common salsa recipes. In this seafood delight, the cilantro balances the fire from those beloved jalapeños with the rich buttery flavor of avocado and zest of lime.

Coarsely chop the shrimp. Place in a large bowl and toss with the cilantro, jalapeño, and onion. Just before serving, peel, seed, and dice the avocados into bite-sized chunks. Add the avocado chunks and lime juice to the salsa mixture and toss gently. Serve with corn tortilla chips. ☀
[Makes 6 servings]

1 POUND SHRIMP, COOKED AND CLEANED, TAILS REMOVED
1 TABLESPOON FRESH CILANTRO, MINCED
1 FRESH JALAPEÑO CHILE, SEEDED AND DICED
1/3 CUP RED ONION, DICED
2 MEDIUM AVOCADOS, RIPE BUT FIRM
JUICE OF 2 LIMES

Chile-Spiced Pecans

I have four pecan trees in my yard. The first winter I lived in my house, those trees produced so many pecans that I decided to shell and sugarcoat them and give them as gifts. The balance between sugar and salt gives a nice crispy coating to these nuts.

Preheat oven to 225° F. Beat the egg white and water in the small bowl of an electric mixer until the liquid is frothy. Fold in the pecans, and stir gently so the pecans are well coated with egg white. Combine the sugar, cinnamon, cayenne, and salt in a small bowl, and sprinkle the mixture over the pecans, tossing gently to coat well. Scatter the pecans on a baking sheet and bake for 1 hour, stirring every 10 to 15 minutes. Remove the pecans from the oven, let cool completely, and store in an airtight container. ✵
[Makes 1 pound]

1 LARGE EGG WHITE
1 TEASPOON COLD WATER
1 POUND HIGH-QUALITY SHELLED PECAN HALVES (SEE NOTE)
1 CUP SUGAR
1 TEASPOON CINNAMON
1 TEASPOON CAYENNE PEPPER
1 TEASPOON SALT

24 MEDIUM MUSHROOM CAPS

1 PACKAGE (1 POUND) SPICED SAUSAGE

8 OUNCES CREAM CHEESE

2 OUNCES MONTEREY JACK CHEESE, GRATED

1 TABLESPOON CRUSHED RED PEPPER FLAKES

2 TABLESPOONS PARMESAN CHEESE, FRESHLY GRATED

Spicy Stuffed Mushrooms

These little bites—tender mushrooms stuffed with a meaty cheese filling—are big on flavor. I like to use Jimmy Dean sausage, because I think it has a perfect blend of spices.

Wash the mushrooms, remove the stems, and pat dry with paper towels. Preheat the oven to 350° F. Cook the sausage in a large skillet until done, drain, and place in a mixing bowl. Add the cream cheese, Monterey Jack cheese, and crushed red pepper flakes. Mix well. Place 1 heaping teaspoon of the mixture into each mushroom cap. Place the stuffed mushroom caps on a rimmed baking pan, sprinkle with Parmesan, and bake for 20 minutes. Remove from oven and let cool for 5 minutes. ✳ [Makes 4 to 6 servings]

2 PINTS FRESH STRAWBERRIES, RINSED, HULLED, AND CUT IN HALVES OR QUARTERS, DEPENDING ON SIZE

6 TO 8 FRESH KIWIFRUIT, PEELED AND CUT INTO ¼-INCH SLICES

1 FRESH PINEAPPLE, PEELED, CORED, AND CUT INTO CHUNKS

4 TO 6 PEACHES, PEELED, SEEDED, AND CUT INTO CHUNKS

AMARETTO CREAM

CHEESECAKE CREAM

1 PINT WHIPPING CREAM

1 TABLESPOON AMARETTO OR OTHER ALMOND-FLAVORED LIQUEUR

2 TABLESPOONS LIGHT BROWN SUGAR

1 JAR (7 OUNCES) MARSHMALLOW CRÈME

8 OUNCES CREAM CHEESE

¼ TEASPOON GROUND CINNAMON

Fresh Fruit and Sweet Creams

Nothing is more inviting during those hot summer days than an offering of sweet, fresh fruit. Rich dipping creams add an irresistible temptation.

Arrange fruit on a platter and serve with Amaretto Cream, Cheesecake Cream, or both. ☀ [Makes 6 servings]

Amaretto Cream

In a chilled glass mixing bowl, whip the cream with an electric mixer. Add the liqueur and, 1 tablespoon at a time, the brown sugar. Mix on medium speed for 2 to 3 minutes, until soft peaks form. [Makes 2 cups]

Cheesecake Cream

In a small bowl, thoroughly blend the marshmallow crème and the cream cheese. Place in a serving bowl and sprinkle with cinnamon. [Makes 2 cups]

Garden Salsa Nachos

Fresh garden produce teamed with rich melted cheese create the perfect nacho. This quick salsa is full of flavor and adds a new texture to this appetizer.

Combine the tomatoes, chile, garlic and white onion in a medium bowl. Mix well. Let stand at room temperature for 45 minutes, stirring occasionally to infuse the flavors.

Preheat the oven on broil. Place the chips side by side on an ovenproof platter. Spoon a half of a teaspoon of the salsa on each chip. Sprinkle the grated cheese over the chips. Broil until the cheese is melted and bubbly, about 4 to 6 minutes. Garnish with the green onion and serve immediately. ☀
[Makes 6 to 8 servings]

Nachos Rancheros

This Southwest ranch-style appetizer has layers of good eatin'. The spicy flavor of the chorizo sausage is at the base of this rich cheesy bean dip. Serve this hearty appetizer on individual plates or scoop it right out of the pan.

Preheat oven to 400° F. Spread the beans across the bottom of a 13 x 9-inch greased baking pan and set aside. Cook the ground beef and sausage in a skillet over medium heat until well browned. Drain the meat and layer it on top of the beans. Spread the cheese evenly over the top, spoon the picante sauce over the cheese, and bake for 20 to 25 minutes, until the cheese is bubbly. Remove from the oven and spoon dollops of sour cream over the cheese. Garnish with minced green onions and serve warm with tortilla chips. ✷
[Makes 6 to 8 servings]

3 TO 4 RIPE TOMATOES, SEEDED, CORED, AND CHOPPED
½ CUP GREEN CHILES, ROASTED, PEELED, AND CHOPPED
1 CLOVE GARLIC, MINCED
1 WHITE ONION, FINELY CHOPPED
½ POUND MONTEREY JACK CHEESE, GRATED
36 ROUND CORN TORTILLA CHIPS
2 GREEN ONIONS, MINCED

1 CAN (31 OUNCES) REFRIED BEANS
½ POUND GROUND BEEF
½ POUND BULK CHORIZO SAUSAGE
3 CUPS CHEDDAR CHEESE, GRATED
1 CUP PICANTE SAUCE OR SALSA
1 CUP REGULAR OR LIGHT SOUR CREAM
3 GREEN ONIONS, MINCED

Pesto Tomato Bruschette

Use a prepared pesto for flavor and ease, and then layer with cheese and fresh tomato. The prepared pesto adds simplicity and a multitude of flavors to this little appetizer.

Preheat the broiler. Spread each slice of bread with a thin layer of pesto sauce. Sprinkle each pesto-covered slice with a teaspoon of shredded cheese, and top with 2 or 3 chunks of tomato. Place the bread slices on an ungreased cookie sheet, and broil for 4 to 6 minutes until each slice is bubbly and brown around the edges. ❀ [Makes 6 to 8 servings]

1 BAGUETTE, CUT INTO ¼-INCH SLICES
⅔ CUP PREPARED PESTO SAUCE
1 ½ CUPS MOZZARELLA, SHREDDED
2 SMALL VINE-RIPENED TOMATOES, SEEDED AND CHOPPED

½ POUND (2 STICKS) BUTTER, SOFTENED

2 CLOVES GARLIC, MINCED

½ POUND MOZZARELLA CHEESE, GRATED

2 GREEN ONIONS, MINCED,

MOSTLY THE GREEN PARTS

½ CUP RED BELL PEPPER, SEEDED

AND CHOPPED

PINCH OF KOSHER SALT

1 LOAF OF FRENCH BREAD, SLICED

LENGTHWISE IN 2 LONG HALVES

Pepper Garlic Cheese Bread

A few years ago, my sister, Katie, brought this bread to a family barbecue. One taste and we were all hooked. This crusty warm bread oozing with cheese and fresh garlic is a family favorite.

In a medium-sized bowl, combine the butter, garlic, cheese, onions, bell pepper, and salt until well blended. Place the bread halves, cut sides up, on a baking sheet, and spread the cheese mixture over each half. Broil for 6 to 8 minutes until the cheese is bubbly and the edges are lightly browned. Slice with a serrated knife and serve warm. ☀ [Makes 6 servings]

¼ CUP OLIVE OIL

1 ½ POUNDS FROZEN WHITE-BREAD

DOUGH, THAWED

2 TABLESPOONS FLOUR

5 CLOVES FRESH GARLIC, PEELED

AND MINCED

2 TABLESPOONS FRESH ROSEMARY, MINCED

1 TEASPOON CRUSHED RED PEPPER

Rosemary Garlic Focaccia Bread

This quick bread is the bread of summer—simple baking techniques that deliver big flavor without stressing out the cook.

Rub your hands in the olive oil before handling the dough. Spread half the flour on a flat surface and place the dough on the floured surface. Sprinkle the remaining flour over the dough. Roll out the dough to a 13 x 9-inch rectangle with a floured rolling pin. Grease a baking sheet using 1 tablespoon of olive oil. Gently place the formed bread dough on the baking sheet.

Drizzle 1 tablespoon olive oil over the dough, and gently spread the oil over the entire surface of the dough with your hands. Keep the dough in a warm place for about 1 hour. It will rise to about 1 inch in height.

Preheat the oven to 400° F. With your index finger, make small indentions in the surface of the dough. Sprinkle the dough with the garlic, rosemary, and red pepper. Bake for 18 to 20 minutes or until golden brown. Allow bread to cool for 5 to 8 minutes, and then cut into squares. ☀ [Makes 6 to 8 servings]

Sweet Hot Cheese Spread

This cheese spread is full of adventurous flavors brought together by everyday ingredients. The sweetness of the pineapple and the zest of the green onion and jalapeño create a delicious but unexpected flavor.

In a medium bowl, combine the cream cheese, pineapple, green onions, jalapeños, garlic, and salt. Beat with an electric mixer for 2 to 3 minutes, and then chill for 1 hour. Place the pecans on a large flat surface. Once the mixture is cold and firm, form it into a ball and roll in the pecans. Coat the entire surface well. Cover and chill for another hour. Place on a serving platter and surround with your choice of cocktail crackers.

Note: If you're not a nut lover, substitute 1 cup of finely shredded sharp cheddar cheese for the pecans. It's a wonderful substitute that gives this recipe a real cheesy flavor. �֍ [Makes 4 to 6 servings]

1 POUND CREAM CHEESE

1 CAN (8 OUNCES) CRUSHED PINEAPPLE, DRAINED

3 TO 4 GREEN ONIONS, MINCED

1 TO 2 MEDIUM-SIZED JALAPEÑOS, SEEDED AND MINCED

2 CLOVES FRESH GARLIC, MINCED

½ TEASPOON KOSHER SALT

1 CUP PECANS, FINELY CHOPPED (SEE NOTE)

Baked Artichoke Queso

I've served this hot cheese spread for years. The green chile and the Parmesan cheese give this creamy spread a hint of spice and saltiness so flavorful that you'll keep coming back for more.

Preheat oven to 350° F. In a medium bowl, combine the cream cheese and mayonnaise with an electric mixer for 2 to 3 minutes on medium speed until well blended. Add the garlic, onion, and green chile, and mix for another 2 minutes. By hand, fold in the artichoke hearts and all but 2 tablespoons of the Parmesan.

Pour the artichoke mixture into an 8-inch ovenproof baking dish, sprinkle with the remaining 2 tablespoons of Parmesan, and bake for 20 to 30 minutes, until the artichoke mixture starts to bubble and is slightly browned around the edges. Serve with tortilla chips or crackers. ❄ [Makes 4 to 6 servings]

8 OUNCES CREAM CHEESE, AT ROOM TEMPERATURE

1 CUP LIGHT MAYONNAISE

3 CLOVES GARLIC, MINCED

½ CUP WHITE ONION, FINELY CHOPPED

¼ CUP FRESH GREEN CHILE, MINCED

1 (8 OUNCES) CAN ARTICHOKE HEARTS, DRAINED AND CHOPPED

1 CUP PARMESAN CHEESE, GRATED

Savory Soups & Salads

There is nothing complicated about creating a wonderful pot of soup or a crisp fresh salad loaded with flavor. Infusing the flavors of Mexico, by adding fresh chile and herbs grown in the region, creates a Southwest flavor that you won't forget. Rich hearty chowders like my Chile Corn Chowder or Baked Potato Chowder are quick, easy, and bursting with flavor. Sopa de Pollo is the best known Mexican-style soup around here, and my version of this flavorful chicken soup takes just minutes to prepare. Good Southwest cooking calls for a lot of fresh produce, not only for salsas but also for salads, or in this case, Salsa-style salads like my Latino Salsa Salad, or Spicy Winter Greens tossed with zesty flavors. Verde Fresco Salad is full of fresh green beans and mushrooms that are lightly steamed and laced with Southwest herbs. Serve any of these soups and salads as a first course or the main meal. It's all quick cuisine—flavorful and fun!

SOUPS

Green Chile Turkey Stew

Spicy Sun Bowl Chowder

Sopa de Pollo

Pinto Beans and Chile

Sopa de Lima

Chile Corn Chowder

Baked Potato Chowder

SALADS

Festive Caesar Salad

Latino Salsa Salad

Verde Fresco Salad

Fresh Basil-Tomato Summer Salad

Spicy Winter Greens

Southwest Bacon, Lettuce, and Tomato Salad

Baby Red Potato Salad

Strawberry and Spinach Holiday Salad

SAVORY SOUPS

½ cup onion, diced

3 cloves fresh garlic, minced

2 fresh vine-ripened tomatoes,
seeded and diced

1 pound fresh green chiles,
roasted, seeded, peeled,
and chopped

2 tablespoons olive oil

3 cups chicken stock

2 to 3 cups roasted turkey, diced
or shredded into bite-sized pieces
(see note)

Green Chile Turkey Stew

This hearty, flavorful soup is a favorite every fall season. I usually prepare it with my leftover Thanksgiving turkey. A savory soup is always inviting on a crisp, cool autumn day.

Sauté the onion, garlic, tomato, and green chiles in the olive oil in a large pot over medium-low heat. Simmer for 5 to 10 minutes on medium heat so the flavors blend and the onions become transparent. Add the chicken stock and turkey. Simmer over low heat for 1 to 2 hours. Serve hot.

Note: This is an excellent way to use leftover turkey, but 2 pounds of roasted turkey breast or chicken will also work well. ✺ [Makes 4 to 6 servings]

2 cans (10 ¾ ounces each)
condensed cream of potato soup

1 can (10 ¾ ounces) condensed
cream of shrimp soup

2 ¼ cups half and half

4 tablespoons (½ stick) butter

3 cloves garlic, peeled and minced

1 ½ pounds medium shrimp,
cooked, drained, peeled,
and chopped

1 tablespoon crushed
red pepper flakes

Spicy Sun Bowl Chowder

I created this chowder for a tailgate segment that my television station was filming for the Sun Bowl game, which is played each December in El Paso, Texas. I wanted something quick and spicy for this rowdy football crowd.

Combine the condensed soups and the half and half in a large pot. Simmer over medium-low heat, stirring occasionally. In a separate skillet, melt the butter and sauté the garlic and shrimp over medium heat for 3 to 4 minutes. Add to the soup mixture and simmer for 10 to 12 minutes. Garnish with the crushed red pepper flakes and chives. ✺
[Makes 6 servings]

Sopa de Pollo

Invite everyone over for a night of savory sopa and cold cervezas. My friends love when I serve up this simple but flavorful chicken tortilla soup. A variety of garnishes make this a fun, festive soup that you can stylize to your taste.

Melt the butter in a large pot, and sauté the garlic and green chiles over medium heat, about 2 to 4 minutes. Add the tomato juice, chicken stock, and chicken, and cook over medium-low heat for about 20 minutes. To serve, place ½ cup of the broken tortilla chips in each serving bowl. Ladle the soup over the chips and, if desired, garnish each bowl with crushed red pepper, cheese, and green onion. ❄ [Makes 6 servings]

2 TABLESPOONS BUTTER

2 CLOVES GARLIC, MINCED

4 OUNCES GREEN CHILES, ROASTED, PEELED, AND MINCED

⅓ CUP TOMATO JUICE

6 CUPS CHICKEN STOCK

2 MEDIUM CHICKEN BREAST HALVES, COOKED AND SHREDDED

3 CUPS BROKEN CORN TORTILLA CHIPS

Optional Garnishes

1 TABLESPOON CRUSHED RED PEPPER

½ POUND MONTEREY JACK CHEESE, GRATED

3 GREEN ONIONS, MINCED

Pinto Beans and Chile

This is the simplest recipe for a pot of pinto beans. The beans are canned—no sorting, no soaking. You can achieve a "slow-cooked" taste by infusing the garlic, chile, and onion flavors with the ham and beans by sautéing them in a bit of lard. Your guests will think you have been cooking all day!

In a large pot, sauté the lard, garlic, onions, and green chile over medium-low heat. Cook until the onion rings begin to soften, about 6 to 8 minutes. Add the diced ham and the beans. Bring the bean mixture to a slow boil. Allow mixture to boil for 6 to 8 minutes. Reduce the heat to low and simmer for 1 hour. Serve in individual bowls garnished with fresh cilantro. ❄ [Makes 4 to 6 servings]

1 TABLESPOON LARD

2 CLOVES GARLIC, MINCED

1 MEDIUM WHITE ONION, SLICED INTO ¼ INCH RINGS

¾ CUPS GREEN CHILE, CHOPPED

6 OUNCES LEAN HAM, DICED INTO ¼ INCH PIECES

3 CANS (29 OUNCES EACH) PINTO BEANS WITH THE JUICE

2 TABLESPOONS CILANTRO

Sopa De Lima

1 MEDIUM YELLOW ONION, CHOPPED

2 CLOVES GARLIC, MINCED

2 TABLESPOONS OLIVE OIL

2 VINE-RIPENED TOMATOES, SEEDED
AND CHOPPED

6 CUPS CHICKEN STOCK

2 MEDIUM CHICKEN BREAST HALVES,
COOKED AND CUBED

½ CUP FRESH LIME JUICE
(FROM ABOUT 5 LIMES)

Optional Garnishes

1 CUP CORN TORTILLA CHIPS, CRUSHED

1 TO 2 AVOCADOS, PEELED, SEEDED,
AND DICED

3 GREEN ONIONS, MINCED

This citrusy broth is light and refreshing. It is perfect for those hot summer nights. Elevate the flavor by adding a layer of tortilla chips, avocado chunks, and the zest of minced green onion.

Sauté the onion and garlic in the olive oil in a large skillet over medium heat until the onion is clear and soft, about 2 to 4 minutes. Add the tomato, stock, chicken, and lime juice, bring to a boil, and reduce to a simmer. Cook, uncovered, for 10 minutes. Serve in individual bowls, and garnish, if desired, with the tortilla chips, avocado, and green onions. ☀ [Makes 6 servings]

Chile Corn Chowder

2 cans (10 ¾ ounces) Campbell's
condensed fiesta nacho
cheese soup
2 ½ cups half and half cream
3 tablespoons butter
3 cloves garlic, peeled and minced
2 (15 ounce) cans whole kernel
corn, drained
2 large zucchini, chopped into
¼-inch pieces
1 cup hot green chile, roasted,
seeded, and chopped
1 cup grated cheddar cheese
(optional)

This is my version of my favorite Mexican side dish. I love the combination of green chile, corn, and zucchini. I created this creamy chowder to reflect those same flavors, all folded into a hearty cheese soup.

Combine the condensed soup and the half and half cream in a large pot. Simmer over medium-low heat, stirring occasionally. In a separate skillet, sauté the butter, garlic, corn, zucchini, and chile until zucchini starts to soften. Add to the soup mixture and simmer for 10 to 12 minutes. Serve in individual bowls. Top with cheese if desired. ❈
[Makes 6 servings]

Opposite: Chile Corn Chowder (left), Baked Potato Chowder (right).

2 LARGE BAKING POTATOES

2 TABLESPOONS BUTTER

1 CUP ONIONS, CHOPPED

½ CUP GREEN CHILE, ROASTED,
PEELED, SEEDED, AND CHOPPED

4 CUPS MILK

3 CANS (10 ¾ OUNCES EACH)
CONDENSED CREAM OF POTATO SOUP

2 GREEN ONIONS, CHOPPED

Baked Potato Chowder

The rich, earthy flavor of the baked potato makes this chowder irresistible. Chunks of potato, green chile, and onion float in a creamy broth.

Bake the potatoes at 350° F. for 1 ½ hours. Remove from the oven, allow to cool slightly, and dice the potatoes into cubes with the skin left on. In a large pot, melt the butter over medium-low heat. Place the potatoes, onions, and green chile in the pot with the butter. Cover and cook over low heat until the veggies are soft. Stir occasionally. Slowly add the milk and condensed soup. Blend well. Bring the chowder to a slow boil, stirring constantly. Serve in individual bowls and garnish with green onion. ✿ [Makes 4 to 6 servings]

Festive Caesar Salad

Here is a new twist on an American favorite. Start with fresh, crunchy Romaine lettuce, tasty artichoke hearts, and bits of bacon. Dress it up with my Lite Caesar salad dressing and you have a festival of flavor. The spicy mustard in the dressing adds a lot of flavor without having to use anchovies or eggs.

Place the lettuce in a large bowl, and then add the artichoke hearts, bacon, avocado, and cheese. Toss gently until well blended. Toss the salad ingredients with Caesar Dressing, and serve. ✳ [Makes 4 servings]

2 heads Romaine lettuce, torn into bite-sized pieces
1 can (14 ounces) water-packed artichoke hearts, drained and quartered
½ pound bacon, crisply cooked and crumbled
1 large avocado, peeled, seeded, and cubed
4 ounces freshly grated Parmesan cheese
Prepared Caesar Dressing or Lite Caesar Dressing

Lite Caesar Dressing

Combine the onion, vinegar, sugar, salt, and pepper in a medium bowl. Whisk in the olive oil and mustard, blending well. Use as directed in the above recipe.
[Makes about 1 ½ cups]

⅓ cup onion, finely chopped
3 tablespoons cider vinegar
½ teaspoon sugar
½ teaspoon salt
Pinch of ground black pepper
¾ cup olive oil
2 tablespoons spicy brown mustard

Latino Salsa Salad

Freshness and color are at the heart of this border salad. Citrus marinades are a favorite on fresh chopped veggies in my part of the world. Serve this versatile salad with grilled steaks or roasted meats.

Place the corn, chiles, bell pepper, and jicama in large bowl, and toss gently until well blended. Add the lime juice and chile flakes to the bowl and mix gently. Fold in the beans and toss until well coated with lime juice. Serve in small glass bowls and, if desired, garnish with parsley or cilantro leaves.
   Note: For added flavor, drizzle 1 tablespoon of my Lite Caesar Dressing over each serving. ✳ [Makes 4 to 6 servings]

1 cup whole corn kernels
3 poblano or pasilla chiles, roasted, seeded, and stemmed
1 red bell pepper, roasted, seeded, and stemmed
2 cups jicama, diced
½ cup fresh lime juice, from about 6 limes (See note)
1 teaspoon crushed red chile flakes
1 can (15 ounces) black beans, drained and rinsed
1 handful Italian Parsley or Cilantro leaves (optional)

Verde Fresco Salad

1 ½ POUNDS FRESH GREEN BEANS,
RINSED AND TRIMMED AT EACH END

1 TABLESPOON OLIVE OIL

1 TEASPOON GROUND CUMIN

½ CUP RED WINE VINEGAR

¼ CUP FRESH CILANTRO, CHOPPED

8 OUNCES FRESH MUSHROOMS, SLICED

2 RED BELL PEPPERS, ROASTED, PEELED,
AND CUT INTO STRIPS (SEE NOTE)

Winter green beans tossed with red bell pepper and mushrooms make the perfect color and flavor combination. The fresh taste and texture of lightly steamed green beans glazed with a hint of chile will brighten up your winter menu.

Place the green beans in a steamer basket over boiling water. Cover, steam for 6 to 8 minutes until crisp but tender, drain, and allow to cool. In a large bowl, whisk together the oil and cumin until well blended, add the vinegar and cilantro, and whisk again to thoroughly blend the entire mixture. Add the green beans, mushrooms, and bell pepper strips, and toss gently until the vegetables are well coated. Salt and pepper to taste. Chill for 30 minutes or serve at room temperature.

  Note: If you wish, substitute 1 jar (8 to 10 ounces) of roasted red bell pepper strips. ❋ [Makes 4 to 6 servings]

Opposite: Latino Salsa Salad (top), Verde Fresco Salad (bottom).

1 POUND PENNE PASTA, COOKED
AL DENTE ACCORDING TO
PACKAGE DIRECTIONS
1 CUP PREPARED ITALIAN
SALAD DRESSING (SEE NOTE)
1 ½ POUNDS VINE-RIPENED TOMATOES,
SEEDED AND CHOPPED
½ CUP FRESH BASIL, MINCED
½ POUND FRESH MOZZARELLA CHEESE,
CUBED
¼ CUP BLACK OLIVES, SLICED
1 JALAPEÑO, SEEDED AND MINCED

6 CUPS MIXED GREENS
1 CAN (14 OUNCES) HEARTS OF PALM,
DRAINED AND CUT INTO
½-INCH SLICES
1 MEDIUM RED ONION, CUT IN RINGS
1 RED BELL PEPPER, ROASTED, PEELED,
AND CUT INTO STRIPS
PREPARED VINAIGRETTE DRESSING OR
LEMON VINAIGRETTE
FRESHLY GRATED PARMESAN CHEESE

¼ CUP FRESH-SQUEEZED LEMON JUICE
⅓ CUP OLIVE OIL
1 TEASPOON DRIED DILL WEED
1 TEASPOON CRUSHED RED PEPPER
1 TEASPOON FRESH GARLIC, MINCED

Fresh Basil-Tomato Summer Salad

This pasta salad is so simple. The key to this recipe is using top-quality, fresh ingredients. Good-quality pasta shells and Italian dressing and the freshness of the herbs, tomatoes, and cheese make this pasta salad a winner.

Cook the pasta according to the package directions, and then drain. In a large bowl, gently combine the pasta and the dressing. Add the tomatoes, basil, mozzarella cubes, olives, and the jalapeño. Chill for 2 hours, stirring occasionally.

Note: Select a flavorful salad dressing that contains olive oil for a better flavor. ☀ [Makes 4 to 6 servings]

Spicy Winter Greens

I like winter salads that are full of surprises. Spices, color, and flavor must fill the senses. Fresh citrus adds zesty flavor while leaving the calories behind.

Place the greens on a large serving platter, and top with the hearts of palm, onion, and bell pepper. Gently toss the greens with the prepared dressing or Lemon Vinaigrette and garnish with Parmesan cheese shavings. ❄
[Makes 4 to 6 servings]

Lemon Vinaigrette

Combine the lemon juice and olive oil in a small mixing bowl. Add the dill, red pepper, and garlic. Whisk the ingredients together until the dressing is well blended. Use as directed in previous recipe.

Note: This vinaigrette adds a tangy flavor to the winter greens listed above. Pour it over a platter of fresh tomato slices and top with fresh basil for another winter vegetable idea. [Makes approximately ½ cup]

Southwest Bacon, Lettuce, and Tomato Salad

Even though this salad sounds like it's full of calories, it's not. Small amounts of Swiss cheese, bacon, and tomato highlight this vegetable medley. I use a favorite light dressing to blend it all together for a fresh-tasting entrée on a warm spring night.

Rinse the lettuce, pat dry with paper towels, and set aside. Combine the corn, peas, tomato, and cheese in a large bowl, toss gently with the dressing, and chill for 30 minutes. Before serving, remove from the refrigerator, toss with the reserved lettuce, transfer to a serving bowl, and garnish with the bacon.

Note: I like to buy precooked bacon. Heat as directed in the microwave, let cool, and crumble. ✤
[Makes 4 to 6 servings]

1 POUND ICEBERG, ROMAINE, OR RED-LEAF LETTUCE
1 CUP CANNED CORN KERNELS, DRAINED
1 CUP FROZEN PEAS
1 MEDIUM-SIZED VINE-RIPENED TOMATO, SEEDED AND DICED
1 CUP PEPPER JACK CHEESE, GRATED
½ CUP SALAD DRESSING, RANCH OR ITALIAN
4 SLICES BACON, COOKED AND CRUMBLED (SEE NOTE)

Baby Red Potato Salad

Potato salad can be such a hassle to make. All the peeling, chopping, and mixing can seem endless. But this one is quick and easy. The dry wine and spicy mustard create a feisty, flavored potato salad.

Boil the potatoes just until they are tender when pierced with a fork. Do not overcook. Drain the potatoes, let them cool to room temperature, cut them into bite-sized pieces, and place the pieces in a large bowl. Add the wine and gently toss until the wine is absorbed. In small bowl, combine the mayonnaise, sour cream, mustard, green chile, and celery. Pour over the potatoes and toss gently. Chill for 2 hours. Let stand at room temperature for approximately 15 minutes before serving. ☀ [Makes 6 servings]

2 ½ POUNDS UNPEELED RED POTATOES
⅓ CUP DRY WHITE WINE OR DRY CHAMPAGNE
½ CUP MAYONNAISE
½ CUP SOUR CREAM
1 ½ TABLESPOONS DIJON MUSTARD
½ CUP GREEN CHILE, ROASTED, PEELED, SEEDED, AND CHOPPED
1 CUP CELERY, COARSELY CHOPPED

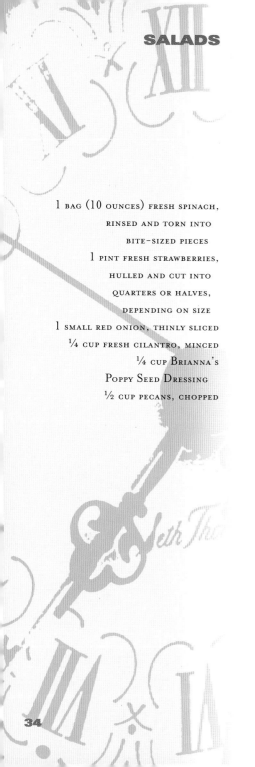

Strawberry and Spinach Holiday Salad

1 bag (10 ounces) fresh spinach, rinsed and torn into bite-sized pieces
1 pint fresh strawberries, hulled and cut into quarters or halves, depending on size
1 small red onion, thinly sliced
¼ cup fresh cilantro, minced
¼ cup Brianna's Poppy Seed Dressing
½ cup pecans, chopped

I promise that this salad will wake up your taste buds. Fresh spinach accented with sweet strawberries, crunchy pecans, and zesty red onions add color and splendor to your table. The tangy poppy seed dressing crowns this salad with an unusual glaze that you'll love.

Place the spinach, strawberries, onion, and cilantro in a large bowl, toss gently, and chill for 30 minutes. Pour the dressing over the chilled salad. Place on a serving platter and top with the pecans. [Makes 4 to 6 servings]

Opposite: Fresh Basil Tomato Summer Salad (top), Strawberry and Spinach Holiday Salad (bottom).

Main Meals

I have found that the focus of any Southwest gathering is the food, and more specifically, the regional flavors and Mexican-style cooking techniques. I have combined these two elements to create dishes such as Sour Cream Enchiladas stuffed with tender chicken, melted cheese, and spicy sauce—rolled and baked to perfection—and Jalapeño Glazed Halibut, Pork Loin Fajitas, and Sizzlin' Southwest Steak, which all take only minutes to prepare. Grilling up tender juicy ribs with spicy Apple Bourbon Sauce or a quick Margarita Chicken is a snap during the warmer months, and the delicious sauces and marinades accent the meat and infuse a full southwestern flavor. Roasting an enticing holiday meat entrée like my Perfect Prime Rib with 7 ingredients or less offers a main meal that is elegant and full of flavor. Or, when your week-nights call for quick and easy meals, try my "one skillet" Chicken Piccata Olé or gather the family around for some finger lickin' Baja Tacos. They are quick Southwest recipes that everyone will love. So save yourself from long days in the kitchen by keeping it simple, Southwest, and seasonal.

RISE & SHINE

Fiesta Breakfast

Chile con Huevos

Southwest Sunday Quiche

Crème Brûlée Pancakes

Pumpkin Pancakes

LIGHT BITES

Garden Quesadilla

Garlic Chicken on Sourdough

Pesto Artichoke Pizza

Chipotle Chicken Pizza

Red Pepper Tostadas

Turkey, Avocado, and Pepper
  Wraps

Pastrami and Pepper Jack
  Wraps

ENTRÉES

Sour Cream Chicken Enchiladas

Margarita Chicken

Crusted Pecan Chicken

Chicken Piccata Olé

Spicy Chicken Stir Fry

Green Chile Enchiladas

Grilled Garlic Chicken

Marinated Pork Loin Chops

Grilled Ribs with Apple
  Bourbon Sauce

Pork Loin Fajitas

Honey Glazed Ham with
  Green Chile Relish

Garlic Rosemary Pork
  Tenderloin

Grilled Tri-Tip Roast

Picante Pot Roast

Gingered Beef Short Ribs

Perfect Prime Rib

Grilled Rib-Eye Steak
  with Jalapeño Salsa

Sizzlin' Southwest Steak

Baja Tacos

Lobster Marinara
  and Pasta Amor

Chile Shrimp Caliente

Jalapeño Glazed Halibut

8 EGGS, WHIPPED

8 SLICES BACON, CUT INTO
SMALL PIECES

1 LARGE ONION, THINLY SLICED

1 CLOVE GARLIC, MINCED

1 CUP GREEN CHILES, ROASTED, PEELED,
SEEDED, AND CHOPPED

2 LARGE VINE-RIPENED TOMATOES,
SEEDED AND CHOPPED

SALT AND PEPPER TO TASTE

Fiesta Breakfast

I love this morning meal. It's my version of Huevos Rancheros. The bacon salsa makes a southwestern breakfast to remember.

Whip the eggs with an electric mixer for 1 to 2 minutes on medium speed in a mixing bowl. Set aside. In a large skillet, fry the bacon pieces slowly until almost done, and drain off all but 1 teaspoon of fat. Add the onion and garlic to the same skillet and brown lightly. Fold in the green chiles and tomato, cover, and simmer 20 minutes, stirring frequently.

In non-stick skillet, cook eggs over medium-high heat. Stir and scrape the bottom of the pan until eggs are cooked through and fluffy. Season the eggs with salt and pepper. Place the eggs on a serving platter and top with the bacon salsa mixture. You can also serve this breakfast salsa over fried or poached eggs. ✳ [Makes 6 to 8 servings]

Chile con Huevos

Our family has been making this fluffy, light, flavorful breakfast casserole for years. I usually make it the night before, saving time in the morning. Serve it with your favorite salsa or try a fresh Pico de Gallo salsa (pg. 8). It is a great way to start your day.

Preheat oven to 350° F., and grease a 13 x 9-inch baking dish. In a large bowl, beat the eggs with an electric mixer at medium speed for about 3 minutes, until they are light and lemon-colored. In another bowl, combine the flour and baking powder, and add the mixture to the eggs. Beat for 2 minutes, fold in the cheeses and the butter, and mix by hand until everything is well blended. Stir in the chiles and pour the mixture into the baking dish.

    Bake for 35 to 40 minutes, or until the top and the edges of the egg mixture have lightly browned and the center is firm to the touch. Cut into 3-inch squares and, if desired, serve immediately with your favorite prepared salsa or fresh Pico de Gallo (pg. 8). ❀ [Makes 6 to 8 servings]

Southwest Sunday Quiche

This quiche is full of layered goodness—cheese, bacon, and onion. It is a no-crust, no-fuss, no-mess egg casserole. Start the night before for the perfect quiche breakfast.

Butter a 9-inch quiche baking dish and place the bread cubes and half of the cooked bacon on the bottom of the pan. Sprinkle evenly with the cheese, and drizzle with the melted butter. In a medium bowl, beat the eggs and the milk with an electric mixer and pour the mixture over the bread and cheese. Top with the remaining bacon and the green onion. Refrigerate overnight.

    Preheat oven to 325° F. Bake for 45 minutes, until the egg mixture puffs up and is golden brown around the edges. Let cool for a few minutes before serving. ❀
[Makes 4 to 6 servings]

10 LARGE EGGS

½ CUP FLOUR

1 TEASPOON BAKING POWDER

2 CUPS COTTAGE CHEESE

1 POUND CHEDDAR OR MONTEREY JACK CHEESE, GRATED

¼ POUND (1 STICK) BUTTER, MELTED

1 CUP FRESH GREEN CHILES, ROASTED, PEELED, AND SEEDED

PREPARED SALSA OR PICO DE GALLO (PG. 8) (OPTIONAL)

5 CUPS BREAD CUBES

12 SLICES BACON, COOKED AND CRUMBLED

1 ¼ CUPS PEPPER JACK CHEESE, GRATED

4 TABLESPOONS (½ STICK) BUTTER, MELTED

8 LARGE EGGS

1 ½ CUPS MILK

3 GREEN ONIONS, MINCED

2 ½ TABLESPOONS BUTTER

1 ¼ CUP FRENCH VANILLA
FLAVORED CREAMER

¾ CUP FLOUR

3 LARGE EGGS

¼ TEASPOON SALT

1 TO 2 CUPS FRESH BERRIES
(RASPBERRIES, STRAWBERRIES, OR
BLACKBERRIES, FOR EXAMPLE)

MAPLE SYRUP OR POWDERED SUGAR
(OPTIONAL)

Crème Brûlée Pancakes

This pancake has the flavor and texture of a rich crème brûlée dessert. Watch it puff up as you cook it before it settles into a rich, thick pancake. Cut it into thick wedges and serve with a sprinkle of powdered sugar and fresh fruit. This is a special-occasion breakfast entrée at my house.

Preheat oven to 400° F. Place the butter in a 9-inch glass pie plate, and place the dish in the oven for a few minutes to allow the butter to melt. In a blender, combine the creamer, flour, eggs, and salt, and blend until smooth.

Remove the baking dish from the oven and increase the oven temperature to 425° F. Spread the melted butter around the dish, pour in the batter, and return the dish to the oven. Bake for 20 minutes. Reduce the oven temperature to 325° F. and bake for 8 to 10 minutes more. Remove from the oven, and let the pancake cool slightly. Cut the pancake into wedges, place each wedge on a serving plate, and garnish with fresh berries. Serve with warm maple syrup or powdered sugar if desired. ❄ [Makes 4 servings]

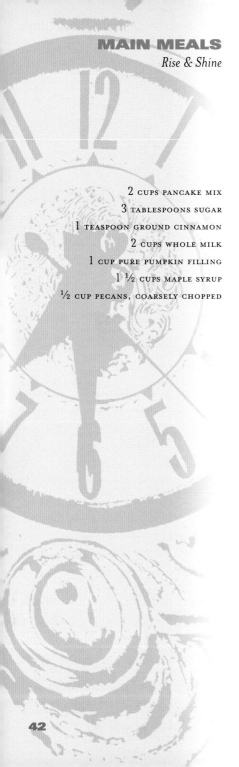

2 CUPS PANCAKE MIX

3 TABLESPOONS SUGAR

1 TEASPOON GROUND CINNAMON

2 CUPS WHOLE MILK

1 CUP PURE PUMPKIN FILLING

1 ½ CUPS MAPLE SYRUP

½ CUP PECANS, COARSELY CHOPPED

Pumpkin Pancakes

This is a wonderful fall breakfast treat. The rich pumpkin and cinnamon flavors are the essence of the fall season.

Combine the pancake mix, sugar, and cinnamon in a large bowl. In a separate bowl, thoroughly mix the milk and the pumpkin filling. Slowly combine the pumpkin mixture with the dry mixture, and whisk until smooth. Add more milk if the mixture seems too thick.

Pour about ¼ cup of batter per pancake onto a lightly greased skillet or griddle over medium heat. Cook until the pancakes are golden brown on the edges and air bubbles appear in the center of each pancake. Flip the pancakes, and cook on their second side until golden brown on the edges. Serve individual plates of pancakes with your favorite syrup and chopped nuts. Keep the pancakes warm in a 200° F. oven. ☀ [Makes 14 to 16 pancakes]

Garden Quesadilla

The sizzle of buttery fresh garlic and natural greens creates an inviting aroma. Fresh spinach and garlic wrapped in rich melted cheese make this quesadilla the perfect light meal.

Melt 2 tablespoons of the butter in a medium skillet and sauté the spinach, onion, and garlic until the onions are almost translucent. Let cool and season with crushed red pepper. Fold the grated cheese into the spinach mixture and spread 2 to 3 tablespoons of the mixture onto half of each tortilla. Fold each tortilla in half to cover the mixture. In a skillet or on a heavy griddle, melt about ½ teaspoon of the remaining butter before grilling each filled tortilla. Grill the quesadillas, one at a time, on each side until golden brown, about 3 to 5 minutes. Cut each tortilla in half, and place the halves on a serving plate. ✳ [Makes 6 servings]

Garlic Chicken on Sourdough

Turn the chicken from the recipe on page 54 into a sandwich big enough for everyone to share. Slices of Grilled Garlic Chicken and red bell pepper are tucked inside a fresh loaf of sourdough bread laced with a tasty mayonnaise. It's a big sandwich with big flavor!

Pull out some of the bread from the middle of each half, and spread both sides of the loaf with the mayonnaise mixture. Layer Grilled Garlic Chicken, strips of the bell pepper, sliced onion, avocado chunks, and lettuce on half the loaf. Place the other half of the loaf on top, and, with a serrated knife, cut the sandwich into 1 ½-inch slices. ✳
[Makes 6 servings]

3 TABLESPOONS BUTTER
½ POUND FRESH SPINACH, CLEANED, DRIED, AND CHOPPED
1 SMALL WHITE ONION, FINELY CHOPPED
2 CLOVES GARLIC, MINCED
1 TABLESPOON CRUSHED RED PEPPER FLAKES
1 POUND MONTEREY JACK CHEESE, GRATED
5 MEDIUM FLOUR TORTILLAS, 8 TO 10 INCHES IN DIAMETER

1 LOAF SOURDOUGH BREAD, SLICED LENGTHWISE
½ CUP SUN DRIED TOMATO-FLAVORED MAYONNAISE
1 RECIPE GRILLED GARLIC CHICKEN, CUT INTO ¼-INCH SLICES (PG. 54)
2 RED BELL PEPPERS, SEEDED AND SLICED IN 1¼-INCH STRIPS
½ LARGE RED ONION, THINLY SLICED
2 MEDIUM AVOCADOS, PEELED, SEEDED, AND CUT INTO CHUNKS
4 TO 6 FULL LEAVES OF RED-LEAF LETTUCE, RINSED AND DRIED

1 12-INCH PREPARED PIZZA CRUST OR
HOMEMADE PIZZA CRUST (PG. 45)
1 TABLESPOON GARLIC OIL (PG. 45)
½ CUP PREPARED PESTO SAUCE
1 CUP MOZZARELLA CHEESE, GRATED
½ CUP ARTICHOKE HEARTS, DRAINED
AND CHOPPED
½ CUP GREEN CHILE, CHOPPED
½ MEDIUM-SIZED RED ONION,
THINLY SLICED

HOMEMADE PIZZA!

Making wonderful gourmet pizzas at home is so simple. Just start with my "home-style" pre-baked crust made from frozen bread dough and brush with some garlic-infused olive oil. If you are really pressed for time, use the pre-baked pizza crusts available in the bread section of your grocery store and finish it off with the Pesto Artichoke toppings, or kick it up with my spicy Chipotle Chicken topping.

Pesto Artichoke Pizza

The prepared pesto adds a lot of flavor to this pizza without the extra ingredients. Add a few extra fresh vegetables, such as sliced tomatoes, after it comes out of the oven for more flavor.

Preheat oven to 400° F. Brush the crust with the Garlic Oil, spoon the pesto sauce over crust, and spread the sauce to the edges. Sprinkle with the cheese and top with artichoke hearts, green chile, and onions. Bake for 18 to 20 minutes or until the cheese is bubbling and the edges are golden brown. ❦ [Makes 4 to 6 slices]

Chipotle Chicken Pizza

This pizza has a hearty southwestern style. The rich, smoky flavor of the chipotle chile perfectly complements the flavor of a prepared barbecue sauce.

Preheat oven to 400° F. Brush the crust with the garlic oil. In a medium bowl, combine the chiles, barbecue sauce, and honey. Blend well. Add the shredded chicken and gently toss. Place the chicken mixture evenly atop the pizza crust, spreading to the edges. Sprinkle the crust with the cheese. Bake for 20 minutes or until the cheese is bubbling and the edges are golden brown.

   Note: Chipotle chiles in adobo sauce can be purchased in 7-ounce cans in the Mexican food section of most supermarkets. ✄   [Makes 4 to 6 slices]

Homemade Pizza Crust

On a lightly floured surface, roll the loaf of dough into an 8-to 10-inch round. Place on a well-oiled, 12-inch pizza stone or baking sheet that has been dusted with cornmeal. Let the dough rest for 5 to 7 minutes before stretching it into a 12-inch round. Bake on the bottom rack of a preheated 500° F. oven for 6 to 8 minutes, until slightly golden brown. Remove and cool on a wire rack. Use as directed above. [Makes 1 (12-inch) crust]

Garlic Oil

Pierce each garlic clove several times with a sharp paring knife to allow the juices to infuse with the olive oil. Place the garlic cloves in the oil, cover, and keep in a cool, dry place for 3 to 6 hours to allow the flavors to infuse. Use with previous pizza recipes, or toss over fresh salad or pasta. [Makes about ½ cup]

1 12-INCH PREPARED PIZZA CRUST OR HOMEMADE PIZZA CRUST

1 TABLESPOON GARLIC OIL

1 TABLESPOON CHIPOTLE CHILES IN ADOBO SAUCE, SEEDED AND MINCED (SEE NOTE)

2 TABLESPOONS MILD BARBECUE SAUCE

2 TABLESPOONS HONEY

2 MEDIUM BONELESS, SKINLESS CHICKEN BREAST HALVES, COOKED AND SHREDDED

1 CUP MONTEREY JACK CHEESE, GRATED

1 LOAF (1 POUND) FROZEN BREAD DOUGH, THAWED AND AT ROOM TEMPERATURE

⅛ CUP CORNMEAL

4 CLOVES GARLIC, WHOLE

½ CUP OLIVE OIL

½ cup prepared salsa

1½ cups ranch dressing

1 tablespoon olive oil

4 sirloin steaks
(4 to 6 ounces each),
trimmed and sliced into
¼-inch-thick strips

2 red bell peppers, seeded and cut
into ¼-inch strips

6 tostada shells, heated as
directed on package

½ head of iceberg lettuce,
finely chopped

1 cup cheddar cheese, shredded
(optional)

Red Pepper Tostadas

This fajita-style tostada is quick and easy. It's a southwestern entrée with layers of flavor and color.

Combine the salsa and ranch dressing in a small bowl, cover, and refrigerate. Place the oil in a medium skillet over medium heat. When the oil is hot, sauté the steak strips until they are well browned. Add the bell pepper strips, and sauté over medium-high heat until the peppers are soft and the meat starts to char. Divide the lettuce evenly among the tostada shells, and top each shell with the meat-pepper mixture. Drizzle the chilled dressing over the tostadas and, if desired, sprinkle them with cheese. ✽ [Makes 6 servings]

Turkey, Avocado, and Pepper Wraps

This crazy little southwestern sandwich will add excitement to any lunch hour. I love the layers of tender turkey, fresh avocado, and roasted red bell pepper all rolled into a wrap full of flavor. Roll it up and enjoy!

Spread a thin layer of the mayonnaise on one side of each tortilla. Place lettuce leaves on each tortilla, and top with a 3 slices of turkey. Arrange avocado and pepper strips on top of turkey slices and carefully roll each tortilla into a cylinder shape. Secure the rolls with a toothpick and cut each in half diagonally. ☀ [Makes 4 servings]

4 FLOUR TORTILLAS, 8 TO 10 INCHES
IN DIAMETER

½ CUP WASABAI HORSERADISH-
FLAVORED MAYONNAISE

½ HEAD OF GREEN LEAF LETTUCE

12 THIN SLICES DELI-STYLE
TURKEY BREAST

2 MEDIUM AVOCADOS, PEELED, SEEDED,
AND CUT INTO CHUNKS

1 CUP RED BELL PEPPER, ROASTED,
DRAINED, AND CUT INTO STRIPS

Pastrami and Pepper Jack Wraps

Summer calls for quick and easy entrées. These southwestern roll-ups are fun and tasty. Spicy cheese, Southwest greens, and fresh produce give these wraps texture and zest. The secret ingredient is the flavored mayonnaise. They really give these summer sandwiches a kick of extra flavor.

Spread a thin layer of the mayonnaise on one side of each tortilla. Place 3 slices of pastrami on each tortilla, and top with 2 slices of the cheese. Sprinkle the cabbage, onion, and cilantro evenly over the pastrami and cheese, and carefully roll each tortilla into a cylinder shape. Secure the rolls with a toothpick and cut each in half diagonally. These wraps can be served warm or cold. If serving warm, microwave each wrap on medium-high heat for 1 minute. ☼
[Makes 4 servings]

4 FLOUR TORTILLAS, 8 TO 10 INCHES IN DIAMETER

½ CUP CHIPOTLE-FLAVORED MAYONNAISE

12 THIN SLICES DELI-STYLE PASTRAMI

8 THIN SLICES PEPPER JACK CHEESE

½ HEAD OF GREEN CABBAGE, SHREDDED

1 SMALL RED ONION, THINLY SLICED

½ CUP CILANTRO, MINCED

1 POUND CHEDDAR CHEESE, GRATED

1 CAN (10 ¾ OUNCES) CREAM OF

CHICKEN SOUP

16 OUNCES SOUR CREAM

2 CUPS COOKED CHICKEN, SHREDDED

1 ½ CUPS GREEN CHILES, DICED

12 FLOUR TORTILLAS, 8 TO 10 INCHES

IN DIAMETER

1 BUNCH GREEN ONIONS, CHOPPED

Sour Cream Chicken Enchiladas

These enchiladas have a definite American twist. The green-chile cheese filling is wrapped in a flour tortilla and baked until crispy. Prepare this entrée a day or two ahead, and then simply pop it in the oven for a "no fuss" dinner.

Set aside 1 cup of the grated cheddar cheese. Combine the soup, sour cream, chicken, and green chiles in a bowl, and reserve 1 cup of the mixture for the top of the enchiladas. Spoon the chile mixture on one side of each tortilla, top with 1 tablespoon of the grated Cheddar, roll up, and place all the tortillas seam side down in a 13 x 9-inch baking dish. Spoon the reserved filling on top of the enchiladas. Top with reserved grated cheese and green onions. Bake at 350° F. for 30 to 45 minutes, until tortilla edges are lightly brown and the filling is bubbling. ☀ [Makes 6 servings]

¾ CUP PREPARED MARGARITA MIX

2 TABLESPOONS OLIVE OIL

2 CLOVES GARLIC, PEELED AND MINCED

1 TABLESPOON FRESH CILANTRO,

MINCED

6 MEDIUM-SIZED SKINLESS, BONELESS

CHICKEN BREAST HALVES

1 LARGE ORANGE, SLICED

2 TABLESPOONS HONEY

Margarita Chicken

This recipe has been inspired by America's favorite cocktail—the Margarita. The citrus tequila flavor makes an incredible glaze for grilled chicken. The olive oil seals in the juices for a tender texture.

Combine the margarita mix, oil, garlic, and cilantro in a small bowl. Pierce each chicken breast with a fork and place the pieces in a large resealable plastic bag, along with half of the orange slices. Pour all but 2 tablespoons of the margarita mix over the chicken, close the bag, and refrigerate for 3 to 4 hours, occasionally using your hands outside the bag to work the marinade into the chicken. Grill the chicken over a medium fire for 6 to 8 minutes on each side, until the chicken is opaque and the juices run clear. Combine the remaining 2 tablespoons of margarita mix with the honey. After you remove the chicken from the grill, brush it with the honey glaze, garnish with remaining orange slices, and serve. ☀ [Makes 6 serving]

Crusted Pecan Chicken

*This is a simple middle-of-the-week entrée. Enjoy the roasted, nutty flavor
of this lightly breaded chicken with the wonderful Asian dipping sauce.*

Preheat oven to 350° F. Marinate the chicken in the milk
for 30 minutes, turning occasionally. Combine the pecans,
breadcrumbs, salt, and pepper in a large bowl. Dip the
chicken pieces into the dry mixture, coating well, and place
them in a buttered 13 x 9-inch baking dish. Drizzle with the
melted butter. Bake for 30 to 45 minutes, until the juices
run clear when the chicken is cut in the center. Serve the
chicken with a bowl of your favorite dipping sauce or the
Asian Dipping Sauce. ❋ [Makes 6 servings]

Asian Dipping Sauce

Stir the teriyaki, honey, and chile in a pot over medium heat
until well blended. Remove from the heat and add the green
onions. Mix well. Serve warm with the previous recipe.
[Makes ¾ cup]

6 BONELESS, SKINLESS CHICKEN
    BREASTS HALVES
1 CUP WHOLE MILK
1 CUP PECANS, FINELY CHOPPED
½ CUP ITALIAN-SEASONED
    BREADCRUMBS
SALT AND BLACK PEPPER TO TASTE
¼ POUND (1 STICK) BUTTER, MELTED
PREPARED SAUCE OR ASIAN DIPPING
    SAUCE

½ CUP TERIYAKI
¼ CUP HONEY
1 CHIPOTLE CHILE IN ADOBO SAUCE,
    SEEDED AND MINCED
4 GREEN ONIONS, MINCED

1 LARGE EGG

3 TABLESPOONS LEMON JUICE

¼ CUP FLOUR

4 CHICKEN BREAST HALVES, SKINNED AND BONED

4 TABLESPOONS (½ STICK) BUTTER

2 TEASPOONS CHICKEN BOUILLON GRANULES DISSOLVED IN ½ CUP BOILING WATER

1 TEASPOON CRUSHED RED PEPPER

Chicken Piccata Olé

This lightly fried chicken has a lemony zest that complements the flavorful sauce spiked with a taste of chile. This one-skillet entrée is great for quick weeknight dinners. I like to serve it with a side of fresh pasta and roasted vegetables.

Beat the egg with 1 tablespoon of the lemon juice. Place the flour on a flat surface. Dip each chicken breast in the egg mixture, then in the flour. Melt the butter in a large skillet and brown the chicken in the butter over medium heat. Add the chicken bouillon liquid, remaining lemon juice, and crushed red pepper to the skillet. Cover and simmer for 20 minutes or until the chicken is tender. ✖
[Makes 4 servings]

2 TABLESPOONS CHILE-FLAVORED COOKING OIL (SEE NOTE)

1 CLOVE GARLIC, MINCED

8 OUNCES FRESH ASPARAGUS, WASHED AND TRIMMED

1 CUP MUSHROOMS, WASHED AND SLICED

1 RED BELL PEPPER, SEEDED AND SLICED

2 TABLESPOONS SOY SAUCE

2 SKINLESS, BONELESS CHICKEN BREAST HALVES, COOKED AND CUBED

Spicy Chicken Stir Fry

The essence of spring is captured in this stir fry with fresh, seasoned vegetables bursting with flavor and color. The quick preparation time will make this a family favorite.

Heat oil in a large skillet over medium heat. When oil is hot, sauté the garlic. When the garlic sizzles, add the asparagus, mushrooms, bell pepper, and soy sauce, and then toss until the vegetables are well coated. Add the chicken cubes, blend, and toss until the vegetables are tender but not overcooked. Transfer to a platter and serve warm.

Note: There are a variety of chile-infused cooking oils on the market with varying degrees of heat. You will find them in the oriental food section of your grocery store. ✖
[Makes 4 to 6 servings]

Green Chile Enchiladas

A few years back, I asked a friend from Mexico to teach me to make a good green-chile enchilada with an authentic Mexican flavor. Imagine my surprise when she showed me how to do this "casserole-style" enchilada with cream of mushroom soup as the base. The key technique is to infuse the flavor of the chile with the soup mix, creating a nice spicy sauce. From time to time, I add shredded chicken for a heartier enchilada dish.

Preheat oven to 350° F. Combine the soup and the green chiles in a large saucepan, add the milk and, if you're using it, the chicken, and slowly bring to a boil over medium heat, stirring constantly. Remove the soup mixture from the heat and set aside.

With kitchen tongs, dip each tortilla in the soup mixture, one at a time. Shake excess soup mixture from each tortilla. Place the first 6 tortillas across the bottom of a 13 x 9-inch pan. Top the tortillas with a thin layer of soup mixture. Sprinkle the mixture lightly with the grated cheese and chopped onion. Repeat 3 times, giving you 4 layers. Bake for 30 minutes until lightly browned and bubbly.

Note: Another option that will result in a nice flavor is to use ½ pound of longhorn or cheddar cheese and blend it with ½ pound of grated Monterey Jack cheese. ❄
[Makes 6 to 8 servings]

1 "FAMILY-SIZED" CAN (26 OUNCES) CREAM OF MUSHROOM SOUP

1 ½ CUPS FRESH GREEN CHILES, ROASTED, PEELED, SEEDED, AND CHOPPED

½ CUP MILK, ANY KIND

2 CHICKEN BREAST HALVES, COOKED AND SHREDDED (OPTIONAL)

24 FRESH CORN TORTILLAS, ABOUT 6 INCHES IN DIAMETER

1 POUND LONGHORN OR CHEDDAR CHEESE, GRATED (SEE NOTE)

1 LARGE YELLOW ONION, FINELY CHOPPED

Grilled Garlic Chicken

½ CUP OLIVE OIL

4 TO 5 CLOVES FRESH GARLIC, PEELED
AND MINCED

1 TEASPOON KOSHER SALT

1 TABLESPOON FRESH ROSEMARY,
MINCED

6 SKINLESS, BONELESS CHICKEN
BREAST HALVES

Optional Garnishes

2 JALAPEÑOS, SEEDED AND CHOPPED
(SEE NOTE)

1 RED BELL PEPPER, SEEDED AND
CHOPPED (SEE NOTE)

This delicious entrée is simple. I serve it in a variety of ways throughout the season. It is especially delicious when served with Spanish Rice (pg. 74) or my Sun-Grilled Veggies (pg. 75).

Pour the oil, garlic, salt, and rosemary in a large resealable bag. Add the chicken to the bag, refrigerate, and let marinate for 2 to 3 hours. Grill the marinated chicken breasts for 6 minutes on each side over medium heat until the juices run clear. Cut the chicken into ½-inch slices. Serve warm with a salad, rice, or your favorite side dish.

Note: I sometimes add fresh jalapeño and red bell pepper for extra spice and color. ❈ [Makes 6 servings]

Marinated Pork Loin Chops

6 (4 OUNCES) BONELESS PORK LION CHOPS, CUT ½-INCH THICK
1 BOTTLE (10 OUNCES) SOY SAUCE
PREPARED MANGO SALSA OR MY MANGO SALSA (PG. 10)

The simple soy sauce marinade offered here salts the meat to perfection. Or, make this entrée even better by topping it with the rich velvety texture of a mango salsa. Select your own prepared salsa, or try my Mango Salsa on page 10.

Place the meat and the soy sauce in a large resealable bag, seal, and refrigerate. Marinate from 2 to 3 hours in soy sauce. Place chops in a lightly greased 13 x 9-inch baking dish and bake at 350° F. for 20 to 30 minutes until the juices run clear. Serve pork loin chops on individual plates topped with 1 to 2 tablespoons of prepared or fresh Mango Salsa (pg. 10) ☀ [Makes 6 servings]

2 CUPS MILD BARBECUE SAUCE

2 MEDIUM GRANNY SMITH APPLES,
PEELED AND CHOPPED

1 SMALL ONION, FINELY CHOPPED

1 CHIPOTLE CHILE IN ADOBO SAUCE,
SEEDED AND MINCED

3 TABLESPOONS CIDER VINEGAR

¼ CUP BOURBON

3 TO 4 POUNDS ST. LOUIS-STYLE
PORK RIBS (SEE NOTE)

Grilled Ribs with Apple Bourbon Sauce

This is a great grilled meat to serve that favorite guy on Father's Day. Slow-roasted ribs slathered with a tangy sauce is a finger-lickin' crowd-pleaser.

Combine the barbecue sauce, apple, onion, chile, and cider vinegar in a medium saucepan and cook over medium heat until the mixture comes to a slow boil. Remove from the heat, add the bourbon, mix well, and set aside.

Rinse and pat the ribs dry, and grill them over medium-low heat for 1 ½ hours, turning every 15 minutes. After the ribs have cooked for 1 hour, test for doneness by using tongs to pick up the ribs. If the rack droops on both ends, the ribs are tender and almost done. Brush the barbecue sauce mixture on the ribs and cook for 30 more minutes. Allow the ribs to cool slightly on a chopping board, make a cut in between each rib, and stack the ribs on a platter. Drizzle ribs with remaining barbecue sauce.

Note: The St. Louis cut is a rack of ribs from which the butcher has removed the long strip of fatty, cartilaginous joints that attach the ribs to the sternum. Cutting off this strip makes the meat more uniform in shape so the ribs cook more evenly. ☼ [Makes 6 to 8 servings]

Opposite: Fresh Roasted Corn with Butter Herb Sauce (top),
Grilled Ribs with Apple Bourbon Sauce (bottom).

2 POUNDS BONELESS PORK LOIN OR CHOPS,
CUT INTO STRIPS ⅛-INCH THICK
1 CUP SOY SAUCE
1 ½ CUPS PINEAPPLE JUICE
2 TABLESPOONS VEGETABLE OIL
10 FLOUR TORTILLAS, 6 TO 8
INCHES IN DIAMETER
PREPARED SALSA OR APPLE-ONION-GARLIC
SALSA (PG. 9)

Pork Loin Fajitas

Fajitas are a fun skillet dish, and they take only minutes to prepare. I created a saucy little marinade with a sweet and salty flavor. These pork fajitas sizzle with flavor when topped with your favorite salsa, or you could make them taste great with my fresh Apple-Onion-Garlic Salsa (pg. 9).

Place meat, soy sauce, and pineapple juice in a resealable bag and marinate, refrigerated, for 3 to 4 hours. Place the oil in a large skillet or wok over medium-high heat, add the pork strips, toss, and cook until the juices run clear, about 5 to 10 minutes. Cook another 3 to 5 minutes, until the meat starts to char on the edges. To serve, fold 3 or 4 strips of pork in a warm flour tortilla and top with your favorite salsa or Apple-Onion-Garlic Salsa (pg. 9). ❋
[Makes 10 servings]

3 TO 5 POUNDS HONEY-GLAZED
SPIRAL CUT HAM
1 CUP ORANGE MARMALADE
4 TO 5 CLOVES FRESH GARLIC, MINCED
½ CUP VODKA
1 CUP GREEN CHILES, ROASTED, SEEDED,
PEELED, AND CHOPPED

Honey Glazed Ham with Green Chile Relish

Dress up your roasted winter ham with this sweet, spicy sauce. The chile flavor has a hint of orange that complements any pork dish.

Prepare ham as directed on packaging in a large roasting pan. While the ham is cooking, heat the marmalade and garlic in a small saucepan over medium-low heat. Add the vodka and green chiles, bring to a slow boil, and boil for 1 to 2 minutes until the relish is well blended. Reduce the heat and simmer for 10 minutes, stirring occasionally. Drizzle the relish over the ham and serve warm. ❄
[Makes 4 to 6 servings]

Garlic Rosemary Pork Tenderloin

The simple rub used in this recipe is full of fresh herbs and spices grown around the Southwest, adding a flavorful crust to this rich cut of meat. It's the perfect entrée for entertaining with ease and elegance.

Combine the salt, pepper, garlic, and rosemary in a small bowl, and set aside. Rinse the tenderloin with cool water, pat dry with paper towels, and place the tenderloin in an oblong baking dish. Generously coat the top and sides of the meat with the cooking spray. This will help seal in the juices. Rub the herb mix on the top and sides of the tenderloin, and spray the meat again to keep the herb rub in place. Wrap in foil and refrigerate for 2 hours.

Remove the meat from the refrigerator 30 minutes before baking. Preheat the oven to 375° F., place the meat in a roasting pan, and bake for 20 to 25 minutes. Let stand 10 minutes before serving. ❄ [Makes 4 to 6 servings]

1 TEASPOON KOSHER SALT
½ TEASPOON CRACKED BLACK PEPPER
1 CLOVE FRESH GARLIC, MINCED
2 TEASPOONS FRESH ROSEMARY, MINCED
1 PORK TENDERLOIN, ABOUT
  2 TO 3 POUNDS
GARLIC- OR OIL-FLAVORED COOKING SPRAY

1 TRI-TRIP ROAST, ABOUT 3 TO 4
POUNDS (SEE NOTE)

2 TABLESPOONS GARLIC SALT

2 TABLESPOONS COARSE BLACK PEPPER

2 TABLESPOONS SEASONED SALT

2 POUNDS WHOLE GREEN CHILES,
ROASTED, SEEDED, PEELED,
AND SLICED INTO STRIPS

Grilled Tri-Tip Roast

This grilled favorite has made its way down the west coast and across the southwestern desert. This cut of meat falls somewhere between steak and prime rib according to my taste buds. The seasoned charred crust surrounds a juicy medium-rare center. It is a great way to grill for a crowd.

Rinse the meat and pat dry with a paper towel. Combine the garlic salt, black pepper, and seasoned salt in a small bowl, and rub generously over all surfaces of the meat. Grill over medium-low heat for 50 minutes, turning every 10 minutes. The roast will start to look like it is burning because of the spices, but it will just be charred. After you have grilled the meat, place it in a small ice chest (12-pack size) for 20 minutes. This seals in the meat's juices and actually continues to cook the center of the roast a little more. When ready to serve, slice the meat very thin. Your tri-tip should be medium-rare. Place on a large serving platter and top with green chile strips. This is a great entrée served with beans, rice, salsa, and tortillas.

Note: Ask the meat department at your supermarket for a tri-trip roast. This cut of meat is the tip of the loin portion of a steer. ☀ [Makes 6 to 8 servings]

BONELESS BEEF ROAST, 2 TO 3 POUNDS

1 TABLESPOON VEGETABLE OIL

1 CAN (12 OUNCES) BEER

3 TABLESPOONS LIGHT BROWN SUGAR

2 CUPS PREPARED PICANTE SAUCE
OR PREPARED SALSA

Picante Pot Roast

Sunday Roast, with its long baking time, serves as a terrific weekend entrée. This lively roast is glazed with brown sugar and picante sauce creating a spicy, sweet flavor.

Brown the roast in the oil in a large pot over a medium heat. Add the beer, brown sugar, and picante sauce. Bring to a boil. Cover and reduce the heat to low. Simmer for 2 hours. Serve warm with your favorite side dish. ❄
[Makes 4 to 6 servings]

Gingered Beef Short Ribs

This is one of those "fix it and forget about it" dishes. Browning the ribs and then slow cooking them adds a nice texture to the meat. The pungent flavor of ginger gives this beef dish a boost.

Place the ginger, garlic, and soy sauce in a resealable plastic bag. Place the meat in the bag, close it, and work the ginger marinade into the meat with your hands. Remove the meat from the plastic bag, place it in a large skillet, and cook over medium-high heat until the ribs are crispy and well browned, about 12 to 14 minutes.

Place the slices of yellow onion on the bottom of a slow cooker. Place the browned ribs on top of the onions, and slow-cook for 4 hours on medium heat. Reduce heat to medium-low and cook for another hour. Garnish with green onions and serve. ❄ [Makes 4 to 6 servings]

Perfect Prime Rib

A prime rib roast can be an intimidating entrée. It is an expensive piece of beef, and many people worry that they will overcook their roast. Like most people, I like my prime rib medium-rare. Here is my version of a recipe that has been floating around the Southwest for many years. It comes out medium-rare and perfect every time.

Combine the garlic, black pepper, seasoned salt, kosher salt, and brown sugar in a small bowl. Rinse the meat, pat it dry, place it in a large baking dish, and generously rub the seasonings over all surfaces. Move the seasoned roast to a roasting pan. Do not cover or add water.

Approximately 3 hours before the meal is to be served, place the meat in a preheated 375° F. oven and cook for 1 hour. Turn the oven off, but do not open the oven door. Forty minutes before serving, turn the oven to 300° F., and cook for 40 minutes more. Remove the roast from the oven, and let it stand for 10 minutes before slicing.

Note: You may leave the prime rib in the oven for up to 2 hours without heat. Plan on about half a pound of meat per person, although I buy a bigger roast because I cut my slices thicker than most people do. ❄ [Makes 6 to 8 servings]

2 TABLESPOONS FRESH GINGER, MINCED

3 CLOVES FRESH GARLIC, MINCED

2 TABLESPOONS REDUCED-SODIUM SOY SAUCE

2 POUNDS BEEF SHORT RIBS

1 LARGE YELLOW ONION, CUT IN ¼-INCH SLICES

4 GREEN ONIONS

2 CLOVES GARLIC, MINCED

3 TABLESPOONS CRACKED BLACK PEPPER

3 TABLESPOONS SEASONED SALT

2 TABLESPOONS KOSHER SALT

½ TEASPOON BROWN SUGAR

1 STANDING RIB ROAST, 6 TO 8 POUNDS (SEE NOTE)

1 TABLESPOON OLIVE OIL

4 TO 5 CLOVES GARLIC, CHOPPED

½ CUP GREEN ONIONS, THINLY SLICED

3 FRESH JALAPEÑO CHILES, SEEDED
AND FINELY CHOPPED

¼ TEASPOON SALT

¼ TEASPOON PEPPER

4 (6 TO 8 OUNCES) HIGH-QUALITY
RIB-EYE STEAKS, EACH CUT
1 ½-INCHES THICK

Grilled Rib-Eye Steak with Jalapeño Salsa

Almost everyone loves a good steak. This grilled steak is a thick and juicy cut of meat that has flash and sizzle. Its spicy garlic filling makes it the perfect southwestern steak. Grill it to a nice medium-rare finish.

Heat the oil in a small skillet over medium-low heat until it is hot. Add the garlic and cook until it is tender. Add the onion and the jalapeño and continue cooking and stirring 4 to 5 minutes, or until the onions are tender. Season with salt and pepper and let the mixture cool completely.

With a sharp knife, cut a horizontal pocket in the center of each steak to within ½ inch of each side. Spread a portion of the garlic mixture inside each pocket, and secure the openings with wooden toothpicks.

Grill over medium heat, covered, for 10 to 12 minutes on each side. Remove from the grill and let stand for 5 minutes. Remove the toothpicks and cut crosswise into ½-inch slices. Serve immediately with your favorite side dish. ☀ [Makes 4 servings]

Opposite: Sun-Grilled Veggies (top),
Grilled Rib-Eye Steak with Jalapeño Salsa (bottom).

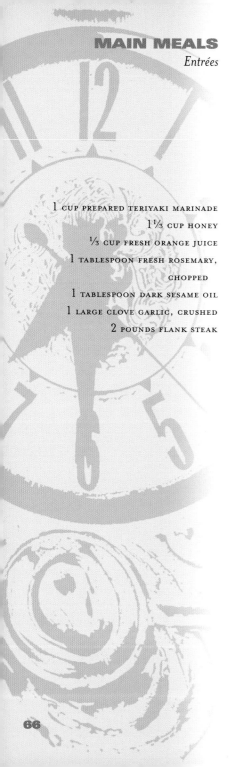

1 CUP PREPARED TERIYAKI MARINADE

1⅓ CUP HONEY

⅓ CUP FRESH ORANGE JUICE

1 TABLESPOON FRESH ROSEMARY, CHOPPED

1 TABLESPOON DARK SESAME OIL

1 LARGE CLOVE GARLIC, CRUSHED

2 POUNDS FLANK STEAK

Sizzlin' Southwest Steak

Flank steak is generally spiced up with chile in my part of the world. However, East meets West with this grilled steak. I love the way these flavors perfectly glaze the steak, combining Asian oils and sauces with southwestern herbs.

Combine the marinade, honey, orange juice, rosemary, sesame oil, and garlic in a small bowl and blend thoroughly. Set aside ¾ cup for basting and dipping. Place the steak and the remaining glaze in a resealable plastic bag and turn to thoroughly coat the steak. Refrigerate for at least 2 hours. Remove the steak from the bag and discard the marinade from the bag.

Grill, uncovered, for 8 to 10 minutes on each side over medium heat for a medium-rare to medium doneness. Remove from the heat and baste with some of the reserved glaze. Place any remaining glaze in a small saucepan over low heat. Carve the steak diagonally across the grain into thin slices, pour the warm glaze over the beef, and serve. ☀ [Makes 4 servings]

Baja Tacos

This Southern California favorite is catching on all over the country. In this tasty recipe, fresh fish is lightly battered and folded into a warm corn tortilla. The creamy chipotle dressing makes these tacos come alive.

To cook the fish, place the flour in a shallow bowl and dredge the fish chunks in the flour. Line a platter with paper towels. Place 2 to 3 inches of oil in a large skillet, and heat the oil until the temperature measures 350° F. on a candy thermometer. Drop 4 or 5 chunks of the dredged fish into the hot oil, and deep-fry for 2 to 3 minutes, until the fish chunks are golden brown. Remove the fish from the oil and fold into one of the warmed tortillas. Repeat with remaining fish and tortillas. Garnish each tortilla with a portion of the prepared or Chipotle Ranch Dressing, and then with a little cabbage and onion. Serve immediately. ☀ [Makes 6 servings]

1 CUP ALL-PURPOSE FLOUR
1 ½ POUNDS FRESH SEA BASS, HALIBUT, SWORDFISH, OR COD, CUT INTO 1-INCH CHUNKS
VEGETABLE OIL
12 TO 14 FRESH CORN TORTILLAS, 6 INCHES IN DIAMETER, WARMED
2 CUPS GREEN OR RED CABBAGE, SHREDDED
1 MEDIUM WHITE ONION, MINCED
PREPARED RANCH DRESSING OR CHIPOTLE RANCH DRESSING

Chipotle Ranch Dressing

To make the dressing, thoroughly blend together the prepared ranch dressing and the sour cream, add the minced chile in adobo sauce, and refrigerate until ready to serve. [Makes 1 cup, enough for 6 servings]

¾ CUP PREPARED RANCH DRESSING
¼ CUP SOUR CREAM
1 TEASPOON CHIPOTLE CHILE IN ADOBO SAUCE, SEEDED AND MINCED

3 TO 4 (6 OUNCES) INDIVIDUAL
LOBSTER TAILS

1 (26 ½ OUNCES) JAR OF PREPARED
MARINARA SAUCE

1 (10 OUNCES) PACKAGE THIN
SPAGHETTI PASTA, COOKED AL DENTE

1½ CUP OLIVE OIL

4 MEDIUM TOMATOES, SEEDED
AND CHOPPED

1 CUP FRESH BASIL, CHOPPED

2 TEASPOONS CRUSHED RED PEPPER

Lobster Marinara and Pasta Amor

Spice up your pasta with some chile and tender chunks of seafood. I love the elegant presentation of this Italian based entrée. Your guests will agree that it is full of color and flavor.

To cook the lobster, fill a large pot ¾ full with water and bring to a boil. Carefully add the lobster to the boiling water and cook 3 to 4 minutes until the shells turn a pinkish orange. Cook 2 to 3 minutes longer to ensure doneness. Remove lobster from the pot when the flesh turns opaque. Allow lobster to cool and then remove the shells. Rinse and chop the lobster meat. Set aside. Place the marinara sauce in a large saucepan. Cook the sauce over a medium-low heat. Add the lobster and continue to cook until sauce is warm.

In a large mixing bowl, toss the warm pasta, olive oil, tomatoes, basil, and crushed red pepper until well blended. To serve, place pasta on individual plates and top with warm lobster marinara sauce. ☀ [Makes 4 to 6 servings]

3 fresh medium-sized limes

1 large clove garlic, minced

1 teaspoon cayenne

1 tablespoon Creole seasoning

2 tablespoons olive oil

2 pounds shrimp, 20 to 30 per pound, peeled (leave the tail), rinsed, and dried

1 tablespoon cilantro, minced (optional)

Chile Shrimp Caliente

Infusing the Creole taste of the south with the taste of chile gives this shrimp dish a new twist and a sassy flavor. My viewers love the 2-step "toss and broil" method I use here.

Move the oven rack to the middle of the oven. Preheat the oven on broil. Squeeze the juice from one lime and set aside. Cut the 2 remaining limes into quarters and set aside. In a large bowl, combine the garlic, cayenne, Creole seasoning, lime juice, and olive oil. Mix well. Add the shrimp and gently toss until the shrimp is well coated. Broil the shrimp, 2 to 3 minutes per side, turning one time. Remove from the oven, garnish, if desired, with minced cilantro, and serve on individual plates with fresh lime quarters. ✽
[Makes 4 to 6 servings]

4 (6 to 8 ounces) fresh halibut steaks

4 tablespoons light mayonnaise

4 tablespoons sour cream

4 teaspoons pickled jalapeño, minced

4 teaspoons bread crumbs

Jalapeño Glazed Halibut

My viewers love the combination of fresh fish and the spicy taste of chile. This elegant dinner entrée can be prepared in just minutes. A simple jalapeño glaze tops fresh halibut steak creating a light and healthy meal broiled to perfection.

Preheat oven to 450° F. Rinse the fish and pat dry with a paper towel. Arrange the fish in a greased rectangular baking dish. In a small bowl, combine the mayonnaise, sour cream, and jalapeño. Set aside. Meanwhile, place the halibut in the oven and bake for 8 to 10 minutes or until the fish flakes easily when tested with a fork. Drain off any liquid. Pat the top of each steak with a paper towel. Without allowing the oven to cool down, turn to broil. Spoon the mayonnaise mixture on top of each steak, spreading it to the edges. Sprinkle with the bread crumbs. Broil the halibut for 2 to 3 minutes, watching closely to avoid burning. Remove when topping is bubbly and lightly browned. ✺   [Makes 4 servings]

Simple Sides

The perfect side dish can jazz up even the simplest entrée. Here I combine some unexpected flavors and ingredients (7 or less, of course!) for some light and tasty side dishes like my Arroz Verde, a Mexican-style rice tossed with fresh herbs and chile. It is amazingly delicious with Chicken Piccata Olé or Garlic Rosemary Pork Tenderloin. Or try a vegetarian dish that can serve as the main course as well as a tantalizing side dish like my Green Chile Relleno Bake. It is a perfect combination of whole green chiles stuffed with fresh cheese and baked in an egg custard. If you get out to the grill this summer, try a few simplistic sides like Sun Grilled Veggies, an array of sliced peppers, onions, and squash brushed with olive oil and accented with rosemary. These simple sides, all with 7 ingredients or less, will turn any meal into a Southwest dining experience.

Spanish Rice

Arroz Verde

Zucchini Salsa Bake

Sun-Grilled Veggies

Green Chile Relleno Bake

Crusted Baked Squash

Roasted Vegetables

Chile Mashed Potatoes

Fresh Roasted Corn
  with Butter Herb Sauce

Baked Potato Buffet
  with Cheese Butters

Red Chile Spuds

2 TABLESPOONS LIGHT OLIVE OIL
½ CUP WHITE ONION, CHOPPED
2 CLOVES GARLIC, MINCED
1 ¼ CUP WHITE LONG GRAIN RICE
1 (8 OUNCE) CAN TOMATO SAUCE
3 CUPS WATER
SALT TO TASTE

Spanish Rice

Is there a secret to making a basic Spanish rice? It is a simple combination of tomato, onion, and garlic flavors wrapped around a fluffy white rice. Try this simple recipe step by step, follow the tips on "texture and doneness," and make the perfect Spanish rice.

In a 10 to 12 inch skillet (with a lid) sauté the onions and garlic in the oil over medium heat. Stir in the uncooked rice and cook until the rice starts to brown slightly, stirring constantly. Reduce heat to medium low. Add the tomato sauce and pour in water. Blend well and cover. Allow the rice to simmer over medium low heat for 15 to 20 minutes until liquid is gone. No need to stir during this time. Check for a soft texture. Add salt to taste.

   Tips on Texture and doneness: If rice does not have a soft texture, reduce the heat and cook covered for another 5 to 10 minutes. Careful not to burn the rice on the bottom of the pan. Remove from heat. Fluff with a fork and serve.

   If the rice does have a soft texture, but liquid remains in the pan, continue cooking the rice uncovered until the moisture has cooked away. Fluff with a fork and serve. ❄

[Makes 4 to 6 servings]

Arroz Verde

Go beyond basic white rice with fresh chile and herbs. This flavorful rice has a hint of green chile and cilantro. It is an interesting side dish for grilled steaks, chicken, or fish.

2 TABLESPOONS LIGHT OLIVE OIL
2 CLOVES GARLIC, MINCED
1 ¼ CUP WHITE LONG GRAIN RICE
8 OUNCES CHICKEN BROTH
3 TABLESPOONS FRESH CILANTRO, MINCED
¼ CUP FRESH GREEN CHILE, MINCED
3 CUPS WATER
SALT TO TASTE

In a 10 to 12 inch skillet (with a lid), sauté the garlic in the oil over a medium heat. Stir in the uncooked rice and cook until the rice starts to brown slightly, stirring constantly. Reduce heat to medium low. Add the chicken broth, cilantro, and green chile. Blend well. Add the water and cover. Allow the rice to simmer over medium-low heat for 15 to 20 minutes until liquid is gone. No need to stir during this time. Check for a soft texture. Fluff the rice with a fork and salt to taste.

❀ [Makes 4 to 6 servings]

Zucchini Salsa Bake

I serve this border-jumper as either a flavorful side dish or a vegetarian main course. The prepared salsa adds a multitude of flavors, and it takes only minutes to prepare.

Preheat oven to 350° F. Butter a 13 x 9-inch baking dish and place the zucchini and squash in the dish. Pour the salsa evenly over the vegetables, and top evenly with the cheese. In a small bowl, combine the breadcrumbs and the butter, and sprinkle the mixture over the cheese. Cover the baking dish with foil and bake for 20 to 25 minutes, until the vegetables are firm, but tender, and the cheese has completely melted.

    Note: This recipe works better with a prepared, store-bought salsa than with a freshly made salsa. I use Pace Picante, medium heat, but try this recipe with your favorite salsa. ✽ [Makes 4 to 6 servings]

2 POUNDS ZUCCHINI,
    CUT INTO ½-INCH SLICES
1½ POUNDS YELLOW SQUASH,
    CUT INTO ½-INCH SLICES
1 CUP PREPARED SALSA
½ POUND MONTEREY JACK CHEESE,
    GRATED
½ CUP BREADCRUMBS
2 TABLESPOONS BUTTER, MELTED

Sun-Grilled Veggies

This has got to be the simplest side dish I've got. The abundance of fresh produce during the warmer months of the year make this a natural side dish to cook on the grill. The roasting technique along with the olive oil and fresh herbs turn these vegetables into a festive feast of flavor and color.

Brush each vegetable piece with olive oil and sprinkle with rosemary and salt. Grill for 10 to 12 minutes, turning occasionally. The vegetables should be firm, yet tender, and have good grill marks across them. ☀ [Makes 6 servings]

2 LARGE RED BELL PEPPERS, SEEDED
    AND CUT INTO ½-INCH SLICES
2 LARGE YELLOW BELL PEPPERS,
    SEEDED AND CUT INTO
    ½-INCH SLICES
1 LARGE YELLOW ONION, PEELED,
    WITH THE TOP AND THE BOTTOM
    TRIMMED AWAY
2 ZUCCHINI, CUT LENGTHWISE IN HALF,
    WITH THE ENDS TRIMMED OFF
¼ CUP OLIVE OIL
2 TABLESPOONS FRESH ROSEMARY,
    MINCED
PINCH OF KOSHER SALT

Green Chile Relleno Bake

This casserole–style relleno dish is a wonderful way to get the flavor of traditional rellenos without frying them. These hearty green chiles layered in a light egg batter and filled with cheese can be served as a side dish or as a vegetarian–style entrée.

1 (27 ounce) can whole green chiles or 2 pounds fresh green chiles, roasted, peeled, and seeded

¾ pound cheddar cheese, grated

¾ pound Monterey Jack cheese, grated

6 eggs

½ cup all-purpose flour

1 cup whole milk

1 teaspoon salt

Preheat the oven to 350° F. Prepare a 13 x 9-inch baking dish with non-stick vegetable spray. In a mixing bowl combine cheddar and Monterey Jack cheeses, mixing well. On a cutting board carefully slice each chile open lengthwise. Clean out seeds and stem. Place 1 to 2 tablespoons of cheese mixture in the middle of each chile. Fold the chile closed over the mixture. Place the stuffed chiles on the bottom of the prepared baking dish.

In a medium-sized bowl, combine the eggs, flour, milk, and salt. Beat with an electric mixer on medium speed, until smooth and lemony in color. Pour the egg mixture over the chiles. Bake for 30 minutes until the center is firm and the edges are slightly brown. Allow to cool and set for 5 to 8 minutes before serving. ✳ [Makes 6 to 8 servings]

Crusted Baked Squash

I'm always looking for ways to serve seasonal vegetables. This is a crispy, creamy side dish that will go with any dinner menu. The chunks of squash are lightly crusted and seasoned with flavor.

2 pounds yellow squash, cut into ½-inch slices

½ pound (1 stick) butter, melted

¾ cup green chile, roasted, peeled, seeded, and chopped

3 cups herb-seasoned bread stuffing mix

1 cup sour cream

1 can (10 ¾ ounces) cream of chicken soup

1 cup cheddar cheese, grated

Preheat oven to 350° F. Butter a 13 x 9-inch baking dish. Place the squash in a large microwave-safe bowl, cover, and microwave on medium power for 3 to 4 minutes until the squash is slightly softened. Drain any excess moisture. Gently toss the squash with the butter until it is well coated. Add the green chile and bread stuffing mix, and toss to coat well.

In a small bowl, combine the sour cream and soup. Slowly fold the soup mixture into the squash mixture, and then pour into the baking dish. Sprinkle the top with the cheese, and bake for 25 minutes until lightly browned and bubbly. ✳ [Makes 6 servings]

Roasted Vegetables

Spring vegetables taste delicious with a rich, creamy sauce. Serve them warm with any of your favorite spring meals.

Preheat oven to 375° F. Place the carrots, yellow squash, zucchini, and asparagus in a 5-quart roasting pan with the water. Mist the vegetables with olive oil spray. Cover the roasting pan with foil, sealing the edges tightly, and bake for 20 minutes. Remove from the oven. Carefully remove the foil and cook, uncovered, for 10 minutes more until the vegetables are firm but tender. Place the cooked vegetables on a serving platter, top with the prepared hollandaise sauce, and serve warm. ❧
[Makes 4 to 6 servings]

1 BAG (16 OUNCES) BABY CARROTS
1 ½ POUNDS FRESH YELLOW SQUASH
1 ½ POUNDS FRESH ZUCCHINI
1 POUND FRESH ASPARAGUS
1 CUP WATER
OLIVE OIL COOKING SPRAY
1 CUP PREPARED HOLLANDAISE SAUCE, WARMED

Chile Mashed Potatoes

This combination of mashed potatoes and green chile comes together and creates a new flavor in potatoes. The minced green chiles give the potatoes a light green hue and an interesting texture. After one bite everyone will want more.

Gently sauté the onion and garlic in the butter in a large skillet over medium heat until the onion is clear and soft, about 2 to 4 minutes. Add the milk and mashed potatoes and stir until heated through. Turn the heat to low, fold in the green chile, and swiftly beat into the potato mixture until the color turns a pale green and the texture is fluffy. Salt to taste. ❄
[Makes 4 to 6 servings]

½ CUP WHITE ONION, FINELY CHOPPED
2 CLOVES FRESH GARLIC, MINCED
¼ CUP BUTTER
¼ CUP MILK
1 ½ POUNDS BAKING POTATOES, PEELED, BOILED, AND MASHED
¾ CUP GREEN CHILE, ROASTED, PEELED, SEEDED, AND FINELY CHOPPED
KOSHER SALT TO TASTE

6 EARS FRESH CORN

¼ POUND (1 STICK) BUTTER

½ TEASPOON MESQUITE-FLAVORED
PEPPER (SEE NOTE)

SALT TO TASTE

2 TABLESPOONS FRESH CHIVES, MINCED

1 TEASPOON GROUND GINGER

2 LIMES, CUT INTO WEDGES

Fresh Roasted Corn with Butter Herb Sauce

Grill some roasted corn for your tailgating fans. Spice it up with a spicy peppered butter and you'll have a fiesta of flavor.

Soak corn, still in their husks, for 1 hour. Peel down to the last layer of husk, and leave that layer and the silk in place. Grill the corn over medium heat for 25 to 30 minutes. Let cool. Peel off the husks carefully, using paper towels.

While the corn is cooking, melt the butter in a saucepan on the grill. Add the pepper, salt, chives, and ginger, and cook until the spices start to sizzle. Brush the butter over each ear of corn and serve with lime wedges.

Note: The markets are brimming with all kinds of flavored peppers. Experiment a little—the chile-flavored ones are very delicious! [Makes 6 servings]

Baked Potato Buffet with Cheese Butters

6 RUSSET POTATOES, 6 TO 8 OUNCES EACH

FLAVORED BUTTERS

These russet potatoes should be slow-roasted in the oven. If you are grilling out, reheat them on the grill, foil-wrapped, until they're piping hot. Then serve them with a variety of flavored butters and cheese toppings. They are a tasty sidekick with any beef, chicken, or fish entrée.

Wash the potatoes and poke them in several places with a fork. Bake the potatoes in a preheated 350° F. oven for 1 ½ hours, or until they are tender all the way through when poked with a fork. Wrap each potato in aluminum foil to keep them hot. Serve with flavored butters. ❋ [Makes 6 servings]

Jalapeño Jack Butter

¼ POUND (1 STICK) BUTTER, SOFTENED
1 JALAPEÑO CHILE, SEEDED AND MINCED
1 CLOVE FRESH GARLIC, MINCED
1 CUP MONTEREY JACK CHEESE, GRATED
½ CUP SHARP CHEDDAR CHEESE, GRATED

Combine the butter, jalapeño, and garlic in a medium bowl. Fold in the cheeses, blend well, and serve on top of a hot baked potato. (Makes 1 ½ cups, enough for 6 potatoes)

Garlic Basil Butter

2 TABLESPOONS BASIL, MINCED
2 CLOVES GARLIC, MINCED
¼ POUND (1 STICK) BUTTER, SOFTENED
1 ½ CUPS MOZZARELLA CHEESE, SHREDDED

Combine the basil, garlic, and butter in a medium bowl. Fold in the cheese, blend well, and serve on top of a hot baked potato. (Makes 1 ½ cups, enough for 6 potatoes)

Red Chile Spuds

Jeff O'Brien offers some spectacular spuds every morning at his eatery in New Mexico's Mesilla Valley. These potatoes are just the side dish to serve with a simple platter of scrambled eggs. Here is a simple version with a big taste that can be served for breakfast, lunch, or dinner.

Fill a large pot half full of water. Bring the water to a boil over high heat. Cut the potatoes into 1-inch cubes. Carefully and gently add the potato cubes to the boiling water. Boil the potatoes until they are soft but firm, about 14 to 16 minutes. Drain thoroughly. Heat the oil in a skillet, and fry the potatoes, stirring occasionally, until golden brown. Season with the salt.

Place the seasoned potatoes on a large ovenproof serving plate, and top them with a layer of bacon and sausage. Pour the chile sauce over the top of the meats and sprinkle with the cheese. Place the plate in a preheated 350° F. oven and bake for 12 to 15 minutes, until the potatoes are heated through and the cheese is completely melted. [Makes 4 to 6 servings]

4 TO 6 MEDIUM BAKING POTATOES

1 TABLESPOON VEGETABLE OIL

⅛ TEASPOON SEASONED SALT

4 STRIPS BACON, COOKED AND CRUMBLED

4 OUNCES SAUSAGE MEAT, COOKED AND CRUMBLED

1 1½ CUPS RED CHILE SAUCE, WARMED

8 OUNCES CHEDDAR CHEESE, SHREDDED

Sweets of the Southwest

Living just north of the Mexican border gives us the opportunity to enjoy many of our neighbor's culinary traditions. Included in this array of Southwest sweets are rich desserts of fresh seasonal fruits and creamy custards, Mexican Bread Pudding laced with cinnamon, and tempting Pecan Pie. Summer in the Southwest also brings hot evenings, which are the perfect backdrop for fresh Mango Martinis topped with a delicious Raspberry Drizzle Sauce and enticing rum-flavored Cherry La Bombas. Or try my Margarita Pie, which infuses the flavors of America's most popular drink, the margarita, with a creamy light filling and vanilla flavored crust. A few seductively sweet endings will leave an unforgettable memory of flavor.

Praline Peach Cobbler

Pecan Pie

Mexican Bread Pudding

Decadent Dippers

Cherry La Bombas

Fresh Mango Martinis with Raspberry Drizzle Sauce

Yellow Ribbon Cake

Strawberries and Mexican Chocolate Drizzle Sauce

Margarita Pie

Bananas Olé

Berry Almond Cream Trifle

Watermelon Sorbet

Praline Peach Cobbler

1 can (32 ounces) sliced peaches
in heavy syrup

Zest of 1 small lemon

1 package (18 ¼ ounces) yellow
cake mix

1 tablespoon fresh-squeezed
lemon juice

¼ pound (1 stick) butter, sliced in
8 to 10 pieces

½ cup pecans, chopped

¾ cup brown sugar

The scent of this cobbler baking in the kitchen is irresistible. My viewers love a down-home dessert with lots of crispy, sweet toppings and lush fruit filling. The brown sugar forms a praline crust around the pecan pieces as this cobbler bakes.

Preheat oven to 350° F. Cut the peaches into chunks (reserving the syrup), and arrange the slices on the bottom of a 9 x 9-inch baking dish. Sprinkle the peaches with the lemon zest. Top with the dry cake mix, spreading it evenly over the peaches. In a separate bowl, combine the reserved syrup with the lemon juice and pour evenly over the cake mix. Place the butter pieces on top and sprinkle the pecans and the brown sugar around the edge of the pan. Bake for 45 to 60 minutes, until golden brown. Serve warm. ✳ [Makes 6 to 8 servings]

Pecan Pie

4 tablespoons (½ stick) butter,
at room temperature

½ cup sugar

3 large eggs

1 cup dark corn syrup

1 ¼ to 1 ½ cups pecans,
coarsely broken

1 unbaked pie crust, 9 inches
in diameter

I loved growing up across the street from the Munk family. Holidays were always a big deal. Mrs. Munk would start weeks ahead, getting out the dishes, planning the guest list, and creating the perfect menu. She paid great attention to detail—but simplicity was her secret. This pie is no exception. I've sampled many pecan pies, and I have to say that this one is my favorites!

Preheat the oven to 400° F. Cream the butter with the sugar in a large bowl. Beat the eggs into the creamed butter using an electric mixer at medium speed for 1 to 2 minutes. While mixing, add the corn syrup. Continue mixing at medium speed until well blended, about 2 to 3 more minutes. Fold in the pecans. Pour the pecan mixture into the unbaked pie crust.

Bake in the preheated oven for 10 minutes, reduce the oven temperature to 300° F., and bake for 35 to 40 minutes more until the crust is browned and the filling is firmly set. Remove from the oven and allow the pie to cool to room temperature. ✳ [Makes 6 to 8 servings]

Mexican Bread Pudding

This rich, layered dessert is one to remember. The buttery flavor and texture of the baked croissants add a new dimension to this custard style Mexican dessert. Crown the bread pudding with a sweet sauce or fresh fruit of the season, and you'll have won your guests' hearts.

Preheat the oven to 350° F. Butter a 13 x 9-inch baking dish. Tear each croissant into small pieces and place in the baking dish, making sure the entire surface of the dish is covered.

Beat the eggs for about 2 minutes with an electric mixer. In a small bowl, combine the sugar and the cinnamon. Add the sugar mixture to the whipped eggs along with the cream and vanilla, and beat for 2 minutes more. Slowly pour the cream mixture over the croissant pieces, pressing them with the back of a spoon so they absorb all the liquid. Bake for 45 minutes until the filling is set. This bread pudding will puff up and then settle as it cools. To serve, cut the bread pudding into 3-inch squares and place on individual dessert plates. Garnish with Vanilla Cream Sauce or fresh berries.

Note: If it is hard to find heavy cream, you can use whipping cream as a substitution. ❄ [Makes 6 to 8 servings]

6 LARGE CROISSANTS
8 LARGE EGGS
1 CUP SUGAR
2 TEASPOONS CINNAMON
3 CUPS HEAVY CREAM (SEE NOTE)
2 TEASPOONS VANILLA EXTRACT
VANILLA CREAM SAUCE OR 2 CUPS
   FRESH-CUT SEASONAL FRUIT

Vanilla Cream Sauce

Beat the cream with an electric mixer until it has thickened slightly, about 3 minutes. Slowly add the sugar and vanilla, and beat until the sugar has dissolved and the consistency of the liquid is thick but not fluffy. Ladle over the warm Mexican bread pudding. [Makes 1 ½ cups]

1 CUP WHIPPING CREAM
⅓ CUP SUGAR
2 TEASPOONS PURE VANILLA EXTRACT

Decadent Dippers

4 MEDIUM-SIZED RED OR GREEN APPLES

8 LARGE ROD-STYLE PRETZELS

1 PACKAGE (1 POUND) CARAMEL
CANDIES, UNWRAPPED

6 OUNCES WHITE CHOCOLATE CHIPS

6 OUNCES MILK CHOCOLATE CHIPS

2 TEASPOONS VEGETABLE SHORTENING

Optional Toppings

1 CUP CINNAMON CANDIES, CRUSHED

1 CUP PECANS, FINELY CHOPPED

1 CUP PEANUT BUTTER CHIPS, CHOPPED

1 CUP DRIED CHERRIES, CHOPPED

1 CUP REESE'S PEANUT BUTTER CUPS,
CHOPPED

1 CUP SNICKER'S CANDY BARS, CHOPPED

Not only is autumn apple season in New Mexico, but it's also snack season at my house. Gourmet Caramel Apples and Decadent Pretzel Dips are delicious treats that are fun to make and eat.

Wash and dry the apples, and place a wooden craft stick in the center of each. Melt the caramel candies slowly in the top of a double boiler, stirring constantly. Dip the apples halfway in the melted caramel, and place on greased foil to cool. Using a spoon, drizzle caramel to coat about 3 inches of one end of each pretzel and place on greased foil.

Meanwhile, spread the candies, fruit, and nuts (optional toppings) on wax paper. Then place the chocolate chips in two separate bowls, each with 1 teaspoon of vegetable shortening, and melt the chips by placing the bowls in a microwave oven at 50% power for 30 to 60 seconds. Continue until completely melted. When melted, stir and then drizzle over the apples and the caramel-coated end of the pretzels. Immediately roll the apples and pretzels in the toppings of your choice. Drizzle remaining melted chocolate over the top. Let cool at room temperature. Slice the apples and serve on a platter with the dipped pretzels. ☀ [Makes 6 to 8 servings]

Cherry La Bombas

1 JAR (16 OUNCES) MARASCHINO
CHERRIES, WITH THEIR STEMS
4 OUNCES HIGH-QUALITY LIGHT RUM
8 OUNCES SEMISWEET CHOCOLATE CHIPS

These little rum-soaked cherry chocolates are a fun cordial to serve at a cocktail party. Your guests will experience a delightful combination of chocolate, rum, and cherry flavors—all in one bite.

Drain and rinse the cherries. Pour the rum into an airtight container, add the cherries, and marinate for 2 to 3 hours. Remove the cherries from the rum, place them on paper towels, and drain any excess rum. Pat the cherries dry.

Place the chocolate chips in a small saucepan and slowly melt them over low heat, stirring constantly. When the chocolate is completely melted, hold each cherry by the stem and dip it into the chocolate, coating most of the cherry. Place each dipped cherry on wax paper to dry. Arrange the chocolate-covered cherries on a decorative serving platter. This recipe is best served the same day. ❄ [Makes about 40 cherries]

Fresh Mango Martinis

2 MEDIUM-SIZED LIMES
6 FRESH RIPE MANGOS,
PEELED AND SEEDED
RASPBERRY DRIZZLE SAUCE

Mangos are an exotic indulgence I enjoy every summer. This refreshing dessert is simple and sophisticated. Citrus laced mango bites drizzled with fresh raspberry sauce offer the true flavors of the season.

Extract the juice from each of the limes and set aside. Slice the mangos into bite-sized chunks. Place the mangos in a large bowl and toss with the lime juice. Chill for 30 minutes. Gently stir and then divide the mangos into 6 martini glasses. Drizzle approximately 2 tablespoons of the Fresh Raspberry Sauce (recipe below) over the mangos in each martini glass. Garnish with reserved whole raspberries. [Makes 6 servings]

4 PACKAGES (6 OUNCES) FRESH
RASPBERRIES, RINSED
¼ CUP SUGAR OR HONEY
3 OUNCES RASPBERRY-FLAVORED
LIQUEUR, SUCH AS CHAMBORD

Raspberry Drizzle Sauce

Set one package of raspberries aside for garnish. Purée 3 packages of the raspberries in a blender or food processor. Press the raspberry purée through a strainer to remove the seeds. In a medium bowl, blend the raspberry purée with honey or sugar and liqueur. Drizzle over the mangos. [Makes 1 ½ cups]

Yellow Ribbon Cake

The Channel 9 staff and I decided that we wanted to name this cake in honor of our local troops from Fort Bliss Military Base. With thousands of yellow ribbons lining the streets and freeways of El Paso, we thought "Yellow Ribbon Cake" was quite appropriate. It is a version of a summer picnic cake my mom used to make when I was growing up.

Preheat the oven to 350° F. Grease and flour a 13 x 9-inch cake pan. In a large bowl, combine cake mix, oil, eggs, and water. Beat with an electric mixer on medium speed for 2 to 3 minutes, until well blended. Scrape the bottom and sides of the bowl with a spatula and beat with the electric mixer another minute. Pour into prepared baking pan. Bake for 30 to 35 minutes until cake is golden brown around the edges and firm in the middle.

Remove from the oven and pierce the entire surface with a fork. Carefully extract the juice from 3 of the lemons. In a small bowl, combine the powdered sugar with the lemon juice, making a thin glaze. Drizzle the glaze over the cake evenly. Slice the 4th lemon into thin slices. Cut each lemon slice in half. When the cake cools, garnish the cake by placing each half slice side by side around the edge of the cake. ✣

[Makes 10 to 12 servings]

1 (18 ¼ OUNCES) PACKAGE
LEMON CAKE MIX
¾ CUP VEGETABLE OIL
3 EGGS
1 CUP WATER
4 MEDIUM-SIZED LEMONS
1 ½ CUPS POWDERED SUGAR

Strawberries and Mexican Chocolate Drizzle Sauce

Chocolate originated in the lowlands of Mexico, where it was used as a beverage. Flavors of cinnamon and almond were used to enhance this delicacy. I often add a coffee liqueur for an extra layer of flavor, creating a rich Mexican-style sauce.

Combine the chocolate, liqueur, milk, brown sugar, vanilla, and cinnamon in a small saucepan over low heat. Stir until smooth and shiny. Divide the berries among 4 serving dishes or stemmed glasses. Spoon the warm chocolate sauce over the berries. Garnish with the almonds if desired. ✣

[Makes 4 servings]

3 OUNCES SEMISWEET CHOCOLATE,
CHOPPED OR MORSELS
3 TABLESPOONS COFFEE-FLAVORED
LIQUEUR, SUCH AS KAHLÚA
2 TABLESPOONS WHOLE MILK
1 TABLESPOON LIGHT BROWN SUGAR
2 TEASPOONS PURE VANILLA EXTRACT
1 ½ TEASPOONS CINNAMON
4 PINTS FRESH STRAWBERRIES, RINSED,
DRIED, HULLED, AND CUT INTO QUARTERS
½ CUP SLICED OR SLIVERED ALMONDS
(OPTIONAL)

Margarita Pie

3 MEDIUM LIMES

4 EGGS

1 (14 OUNCES) CAN SWEETENED
CONDENSED MILK

⅓ CUP PREPARED MARGARITA MIX

3 DROPS GREEN FOOD COLORING

1 (9 INCH) PREPARED VANILLA-FLAVORED
COOKIE CRUMB CRUST (SEE NOTE)

1 (8 OUNCES) CONTAINER OF
NON-DAIRY WHIPPED TOPPING

We infuse the wonderful flavor of margaritas in almost every aspect of our cuisine along the border, and dessert is no exception. I have been on a quest to make the perfect margarita pie—not too tart, not too sweet. Here is what I think is the perfect margarita pie, not only because of its flavor but also the ease of preparation.

Preheat oven to 350° F. Carefully extract the juice from 2 of the limes (this should produce about 4 tablespoons of lime juice) and set aside. Discard the peels. Slice the remaining lime into thin slices and set aside. In a medium-sized mixing bowl, beat 2 whole eggs and 2 egg yolks together with an electric mixer until the mixture is a lemony-yellow color. Discard or save the remaining egg whites for another recipe. Add the lime juice, condensed milk, margarita mix, and food coloring to the egg mixture and beat on medium speed for 2 to 3 minutes until the mixture slightly thickens. Pour into the prepared pie shell and bake for 25 minutes until the center of the pie is firm. Remove from the oven and let cool for 10 minutes. Top with whipped cream and a slice of lime and serve.

Note: Look for the vanilla-flavored cookie crumb crust near the graham cracker crusts in the baking section of your favorite grocery store. ※ [Makes 6 servings]

Bananas Olé

½ POUND (1 STICK) BUTTER
¾ CUP PACKED DARK BROWN SUGAR
2 TABLESPOONS HALF AND HALF CREAM
4 BANANAS, PEELED AND CUT INTO
¼-INCH SLICES
1 QUART HIGH-QUALITY VANILLA
ICE CREAM OR FROZEN YOGURT
SWEET TORTILLA CUPS

My son, Daniel, and I created this mouthwatering dessert of crisp cinnamon cups filled with vanilla ice cream and sliced bananas floating in a rich caramel butter sauce. And since presentation is everything, we do the tortilla cups on nights we entertain. Every so often, though, my kids and I prepare just the bananas and serve the mixture over big scoops of smooth ice cream. Either way this dessert is delicious!

Melt the butter in a medium saucepan, add the sugar, and bring to a slow boil over medium heat, stirring constantly. Boil for 4 to 5 minutes. Reduce the heat, slowly add the half and half, and stir to blend well. Continue cooking and stirring for 2 to 3 minutes. Remove the pan from the heat. Gently fold the banana slices into the sauce. Serve over scoops of ice cream in individual bowls or in tortilla cups (recipe below). [Makes 6 servings]

½ CUP SUGAR
1 TEASPOON GROUND CINNAMON
PINCH OF NUTMEG
6 FLOUR TORTILLAS, 8 TO 10 INCHES
IN DIAMETER
COOKING SPRAY

Sweet Tortilla Cups

Preheat the oven to 400° F. Combine the sugar, cinnamon, and nutmeg in a small bowl. Spray both sides of each tortilla with cooking spray. Gently fold the tortillas into 6-ounce, ovenproof custard cups. Place on a baking sheet and sprinkle each cup-shaped tortilla with 1 teaspoon of the cinnamon-sugar mixture. Bake for 20 to 25 minutes or until golden brown. Remove the tortillas from the custard cups when the tortillas are slightly cooled, and then let cool completely. Place one scoop of ice cream in each tortilla cup and top with warm banana caramel sauce. [Makes 6 tortilla cups]

Berry Almond Cream Trifle

My girlfriend turned me on to this cool dessert a few years ago. It became the "signature" dessert for our neighborhood that spring. Delicate slices of cake and fresh berries tucked between layers of rich cream are a favorite with my friends and family.

Cut the cake into 1-inch cubes, using a serrated knife, and place them in a large resealable bag to keep them fresh. Set aside. Pour the milk and the instant pudding into a large mixing bowl, and whip the pudding and the milk with an electric mixer until well blended. Fold in the whipped topping and the almond extract, and blend well.

Place a layer of cake cubes in a glass serving bowl or trifle bowl. Top with half the strawberries and blueberries. Spread half the cream mixture over the top. Repeat with the remaining cake cubes, strawberries, blueberries, and cream. Refrigerate for 2 to 3 hours. 🦋 [Makes 6 to 8 servings]

1 (10 ½ OUNCES) PREPARED SQUARE ANGEL-FOOD CAKE

2 CUPS COLD WHOLE MILK

1 BOX (3 ¼ OUNCES) INSTANT VANILLA PUDDING

1 CONTAINER (8 OUNCES) WHIPPED NON-DAIRY TOPPING, SUCH AS COOL WHIP

1 TEASPOON PURE ALMOND EXTRACT

2 CUPS FRESH STRAWBERRIES, HULLED AND QUARTERED

1 CUP FRESH BLUEBERRIES

Watermelon Sorbet

Make this recipe with the kids. They will have a blast trying to get the seeds out of that watermelon, and they will watch in amazement as this favorite summer fruit turns into a favorite summer sorbet.

Bring the water and sugar to a boil in a medium saucepan over high heat, stirring until the sugar dissolves. Once the sugar has dissolved, remove the pan from the heat. Cool completely.

Process the sugar syrup and the watermelon in small batches in a blender until smooth. Pour the watermelon mixture into a large bowl, stir in the lemonade concentrate, cover, and chill for 2 hours. Pour the mixture into the freezer container of a 1-gallon electric ice cream maker and process the ice cream mixture according to the manufacturer's instructions. For best results, make a day ahead and freeze overnight until firm. ☀ [Makes 6 to 8 servings]

4 CUPS WATER

2 CUPS SUGAR

8 CUPS WATERMELON, SEEDED AND CHOPPED

1 CAN (6 OUNCES) PINK LEMONADE CONCENTRATE, THAWED AND UNDILUTED

Lively Libations

My viewers enjoy simple, innovative cocktails—interesting and flavorful drinks that make every Southwest celebration complete. Dive into a Michilada, a Mexican beer cocktail laced with fresh lime juice, or a thirst-quenching green apple-flavored martini. A real crowd-pleaser is the Champagne Bar, which allows your guests to satisfy their own tastes with accents of fresh fruit. And of course, America's favorite cocktail is the most important part of this collection. Choose from a classic frosty margarita or, my favorite, the Pink Cadillac Margarita. Team any of these wonderful libations with my simple Southwest fare and you will have a fiesta like no other!

Michilada

Prioska

Sangria Spritzer

Pink Cadillac Margarita

Big Apple Martini

Cactus Colada Martini

Mexican Madras Martini

Sunny Champagne Punch

Sunshine Breakfast Cocktail

Bumble Bee

Margarita Classico

Champagne Bar

Electric Pink Lemonade

Michilada

¼ cup fresh lime juice

Cracked ice

1 bottle (12 ounces) Mexican beer, such as Corona, Pacifico, or Dos Equis

1 or 2 slices of fresh lime

This cerveza cocktail takes the "beer with a twist of lime" idea to the next level. Adding fresh fruit juice to your favorite Mexican beer creates a light and refreshing cocktail served on the rocks.

Pour the lime juice into a tall glass half full of cracked ice. Top with half the beer. Garnish with a few floating lime slices and serve. Add the remaining beer to the glass as needed. ❋
[Makes 1 serving]

Prioska

This refreshing libation has a bittersweet yet tangy edge to it. A high-quality vodka is essential for infusing the citrusy flavor of this cocktail, a popular drink in South America.

Quarter the lime. Place the lime quarters and the sugar in a rocks glass and mash with a wooden spoon or fork. Add the vodka, and pack the glass with 1 cup of the cracked ice. Pour into shaker, shake well, and strain back into the rocks glass. Top it with the remaining cracked ice and let sit for 2 to 3 minutes before serving. ❄ [Makes 1 serving]

2 MEDIUM LIMES
2 TEASPOONS SUGAR
1 ½ OUNCES VODKA
2 CUPS CRACKED ICE

Sangria Spritzer

Traditional Mexican Sangrias combine various fruit juices and can be quite a production. Whip up a quick pitcher of this Sangria by combining a full bodied, fruity zinfandel with a light lemony flavored soda. Garnish with some fresh fruit and Olé!

Combine the Zinfandel and the Fresca in a large glass pitcher. Add the orange, lemon, and lime slices. Squeeze juice from the lime halves into the sangria. Serve in Collins glasses half filled with cracked ice. ☀ [Makes 4 to 6 servings]

1 BOTTLE (750 ML.) RASPBERRY ZINFANDEL
4 CANS (11.5 OUNCES EACH) FRESCA (NO OTHER BRAND WILL DO)
1 MEDIUM ORANGE, SLICED
1 MEDIUM LEMON, SLICED
1 LIME, SLICED
1 LIME, CUT IN HALF
CRACKED ICE

Pink Cadillac Margarita

1 bottle (1.75 liters) margarita mix (see note)
12 ounces gold tequila
⅓ cup grenadine
Cracked ice
4 to 5 limes
Kosher salt

Ahhh, the Pink Cadillac Margarita, my signature drink! This is a great way to serve margaritas to a crowd. I use pre-made margarita mix as the base. This speeds up the preparation time before and during a party. It's a beautiful punch when served in a large, distinctive glass pitcher with cracked ice and sliced lime.

Combine the margarita mix and the tequila in your serving bowl and add the grenadine. Cut 2 of the limes into thin slices and add to the mix. Add lots of cracked ice. Cut the remaining limes into wedges. Rub the rims of each of 4 to 6 highball glasses with a lime wedge. Place the salt on a flat surface and dip the moistened rim of each glass into the salt. Fill each glass with ice, pour some of the margarita mix into each glass, and garnish each drink with a lime wedge.

Note: There are many good margarita mixes on the market. Use a high-quality mix with a medium sweet-sour balance. ☀
[Makes 4 to 6 servings]

Big Apple Martini

1 ounce high-quality vodka
1 ounce green apple-flavored liqueur or schnapps
Cracked ice
Splash of diet lemon-lime soda
1 wafer-thin slice of Granny Smith apple

New Mexico has a small, but luscious apple crop that is harvested every fall. There are also fun apple festivals that highlight the season. Fun—that's what this fruity martini is. The Big Apple is crisp, tangy, and refreshing with a splash of soda to bubble it up.

Pour the vodka and the liqueur in a cocktail shaker half-filled with cracked ice. Shake well and strain into a martini glass. Add a splash of soda. Float the apple slice on top. ❀
[Makes 1 serving]

Opposite: Pink Cadillac Margarita.

1 OUNCE TEQUILA
1 OUNCE ORANGE JUICE
1 OUNCE CRANBERRY JUICE
SPLASH FRESH LIME JUICE
CRACKED ICE

Cactus Colada Martini

This Southwest elixir has a smooth tropical twist. Shake it up by trading the rum for tequila and adding a splash of lime. Relax and enjoy this colada with a kick.

Pour the tequila, coconut milk, and pineapple juice in a shaker half filled with the cracked ice. Shake only a couple of times and strain into a martini glass. Add a splash of lime and garnish with coconut. ❋ [Makes 1 serving]

½ OUNCE GOLD TEQUILA
1 OUNCE SWEETENED CREAM OF
COCONUT MILK
1 ½ OUNCES PINEAPPLE JUICE
1 TEASPOON FRESH LIME JUICE
1 TEASPOON SWEETENED
COCONUT FLAKES

Mexican Madras Martini

This summer martini is light with a fruity flavor. Infusing cranberry and orange juice gives a sweet foundation for this fun martini.

Pour the tequila, orange juice, cranberry juice, and lime juice into a shaker half filled with cracked ice. Shake well, and strain into a unique martini glass. ☀ [Makes 1 serving]

Sunny Champagne Punch

This sparkling punch serves up a delightful flavor on a hot summer day. The light citrusy flavor paired with a high-quality wine and Champagne is the essence of summer entertaining.

Combine orange juice and lemonade concentrates in a large punch bowl. Add the wine and mix well. Float the lemon slices in the punch bowl. Just before serving, add the Champagne to the wine mixture and blend well. Place a couple of raspberries in each serving glass and fill with the punch. ☀
[Makes 6 to 8 servings]

⅓ CUP FROZEN ORANGE JUICE CONCENTRATE, THAWED AND UNDILUTED

¼ CUP FROZEN LEMONADE CONCENTRATE, THAWED AND UNDILUTED

1 BOTTLE (750 ML.) DRY WHITE WINE, CHILLED

1 LARGE LEMON, SLICED

1 BOTTLE (750 ML.) CHAMPAGNE, CHILLED

1 PINT FRESH RASPBERRIES

Sunshine Breakfast Cocktail

I was never a big fan of orange juice until I tasted this drink. The combination of vanilla and orange lends a smooth, sweet flavor to this early-morning starter.

Combine orange juice, water, sugar, milk, and vanilla in a blender. Process for 1 to 2 minutes, until ingredients are well blended. Add the cracked ice, and blend for 2 to 3 minutes more, until the mixture is slushy. Pour into stemmed glasses and garnish with fresh mint. ✾ [Makes 4 to 6 servings]

1 CAN (6 OUNCES) ORANGE JUICE CONCENTRATE

1 ½ CUPS WATER

¾ CUP SUGAR

½ CUP MILK

1 TEASPOON PURE VANILLA EXTRACT

5 CUPS CRACKED ICE

FRESH MINT LEAVES

Bumble Bee

3 TO 4 OUNCES FRESH SQUEEZED
ORANGE JUICE
CRACKED ICE
½ OUNCE GRENADINE
1 CAN (11.5 OUNCES) LEMON-LIME SODA

My kids love when I take the time to fix them a special drink, especially in a stemmed glass. They actually created this refreshing cocktail themselves, and now it is a favorite among their friends.

Fill a large stemmed glass ¾ full with cracked ice. Pour in the orange juice. Add the grenadine, watching it sink right to the bottom. Top it off with 3 to 4 ounces of soda. ❈
[Makes 1 serving]

Margarita Classico

2 LIMES, CUT INTO WEDGES
KOSHER SALT
6 OUNCES FROZEN LIMEADE CONCENTRATE
¾ CUP TEQUILA
1 ½ OUNCES ORANGE-FLAVORED
LIQUEUR, SUCH AS TRIPLE SEC,
COINTREAU, OR GRAND MARNIER
¾ CUP LIGHT BEER
5 CUPS CRACKED ICE

This is the perfect classic frozen margarita, neither too tart nor too sweet. Pour yourself a frosty one, go out on the patio, and enjoy the changing colors of the leaves.

Rub the rim of each of 4 margarita glasses with a lime wedge, pour the salt on a flat surface, and dip the moistened rim of each glass into the salt. Shake off any excess salt. Combine the limeade, tequila, liqueur, beer, and ice in a blender. Blend for 2 to 3 minutes until slushy, pour margaritas into each glass, and garnish each with a lime wedge. ❈
[Makes 4 servings]

Champagne Bar

Creating a Champagne bar is fun and adds excitement to any gathering. Start with two different styles of Champagne or sparkling white wine for your guests (one should be drier, the other fuller and fruitier). Layering the Champagne or sparkling wine with a variety of fruit juices, nectars, and liqueurs creates a fun showcase of flavors.

Set 6 Champagne glasses and a couple of shot glasses on a tray. Pour each wine glass half full with your guest's choice of Champagne or sparkling wine. Offer each guest the opportunity to add a shot of one of the nectars, juices, or liqueurs. Garnish with the fresh fruit if desired.

    Note: Champagne is a sparkling white wine that comes from the Champagne region of France. A sparkling white wine from somewhere else is called just that, "sparkling white wine." It does not have to be French to be good. Many vintners produce exceptional sparkling white wines from California and New Mexico. ❄ [Makes 6 servings]

1 BOTTLE (750 ML.) DRY CHAMPAGNE OR SPARKLING WINE (SEE NOTE)

1 BOTTLE (750 ML.) FRUITY CHAMPAGNE OR SPARKLING WINE (SEE NOTE)

2 CUPS STRAWBERRY-KIWI FRUIT NECTAR

2 CUPS PEACH OR PEAR FRUIT NECTAR

2 CUPS FRESH-SQUEEZED ORANGE JUICE

2 CUPS PINEAPPLE JUICE

FRUIT-FLAVORED LIQUEUR, SUCH AS RASPBERRY OR BLACKBERRY

Optional fresh fruit garnishes

12 TO 16 OUNCES OF FRESH SEASONAL FRUIT, SUCH AS BLACKBERRIES, STRAWBERRIES, RASPBERRIES, PINEAPPLE, OR MANGO CHUNKS

Electric Pink Lemonade

Summertime is lemonade time—only this is lemonade that the adults can really enjoy. Flavored vodkas intensify the refreshing citrus taste in this wonderful cocktail.

Pour vodka, grenadine, and lemonade into a large shaker half filled with ice. Cover and shake until well blended. Pour cocktail and ice into a tall glass and garnish with a slice of lime. ☀ [Makes 1 serving]

1 ¼ OUNCES LEMON-FLAVORED VODKA

¾ OUNCE GRENADINE

4 OUNCES PINK LEMONADE

CRACKED ICE

1 LIME WEDGE, FOR GARNISH

Seasonal Selections

Spring ❦

Pico de Gallo

Sweet Hot Cheese Spread

Pesto Tomato Bruschette

Baked Potato Chowder

Southwest Bacon, Lettuce, and Tomato Salad

Strawberry and Spinach Holiday Salad

Chile con Huevos

Southwest Sunday Quiche

Pesto, Artichoke, and Red Onion Pizza

Chipotle Chicken Pizza

Red Pepper Tostadas

Chicken Piccata Olé

Spicy Chicken Stir-Fry

Chile Shrimp Caliente

Arroz Verde

Zucchini Salsa Bake

Roasted Vegetables

Yellow Ribbon Cake

Strawberries and Mexican Chocolate

Drizzle Sauce

Berry Almond Cream Trifle

Big Apple Martini

Sunshine Breakfast Cocktail

Summer ☼

Fresh Salsa Verde

Sassy Shrimp Salsa

Black Bean Basil Salsa

Mango Salsa

Fresh Fruit and Sweet Creams

Garden Salsa Nachos

Pepper Garlic Cheese Bread

Rosemary Garlic Focaccia Bread

Sopa de Lima

Fresh Basil-Tomato Summer Salad

Baby Red Potato Salad

Pastrami and Pepper Jack Wraps

Turkey Avocado & Pepper Wraps

Margarita Chicken

Grilled Ribs with Apple Bourbon Sauce

Pork Loin Chops

Grilled Tri-Tip Roast

Grilled Rib-Eye Steak with Jalapeño Salsa

Sizzlin' Southwest Steak

Lobster Marinara and Pasta Amor

Baja Tacos

Fresh Roasted Corn

Sun-Grilled Veggies

Red Chile Spuds

Fresh Mango Martinis

Bananas Olé

Watermelon Sorbet

Pink Cadillac Margarita

Sangria Spritzer

Mexican Madras Martini

Sunny Champagne Punch

Electric Pink Lemonade

Seasonal Selections

Autumn ❋

Southwest Snack Mix
Apple-Onion-Garlic Salsa
Nachos Rancheros
Spicy Stuffed Mushrooms
Chile Corn Chowder
Green Chile Turkey Stew
Spicy Sun Bowl Chowder
Festive Caesar Salad
Latino Salsa Salad
Fiesta Breakfast
Pumpkin Pancakes
Garden Quesadilla
Garlic Chicken on Sourdough
Sour Cream Chicken Enchiladas
Crusted Pecan Chicken
Grilled Garlic Chicken
Pork Loin Fajitas
Gingered Beef Short Ribs
Jalapeño Glazed Halibut
Green Chile Relleno Bake
Crusted Baked Squash
Baked Potato Buffet
with Cheese Butters
Margarita Pie
Praline Peach Cobbler
Decadent Dippers
Michilada
Margarita Classico
Bumble Bee

Winter ❄

Chile-Spiced Pecans
Baked Artichoke Queso
Sopa de Pollo
Pinto Beans and Chile
Verde Fresco Salad
Spicy Winter Greens
Oven-Baked Crème Brûlée Pancake
Green-Chile Enchiladas
Garlic Rosemary Pork Tenderloin
Honey Glazed Ham with Green Chile Relish
Perfect Prime Rib
Picante Pot Roast
Spanish Rice
Chile Mashed Potatoes
Pecan Pie
Cherry La Bombas
Mexican Bread Pudding
Prioska
Cactus Colada Martini
Champagne Bar

Index

Note: italic page numbers indicate photographs.

Amaretto Cream, 14
Appetizers
    Amaretto Cream, 14
    Baked Artichoke Queso, 19
    Cheesecake Cream, 14
    Fresh Fruit and Sweet Creams, 14
    Garden Salsa Nachos, 15
    Nachos Rancheros, 15
    Pepper Garlic Cheese Bread, 18
    Pesto Tomato Bruschette, *16*, 17
    Rosemary Garlic Focaccia Bread, 18
    Spicy Stuffed Mushrooms, *12, 13*
    Sweet Hot Cheese Spread, 19
Apple-Onion-Garlic Salsa, 9
Arroz Verde, 74
Artichokes, 19
Asian Dipping Sauce, 51
Autumn dishes, 107
Avocado, 48, *48*

Baby Red Potato Salad, 33
Bacon
    Fiesta Breakfast, 38, *38*
    Southwest Bacon, Lettuce, and
        Tomato Salad, 33
Baja Tacos, 67
Baked Artichoke Queso, 19
Baked Potato Buffet with Cheese Butters, 80
Baked Potato Chowder, 27, 28
Bananas Olé, 94
Basil, 10
Beans
    Black Bean Basil Salsa, 10
    Pinto Beans and Chile, 23
Beef
    Gingered Beef Short Ribs, 63
    Grilled Rib-Eye Steak with Jalapeño
        Salsa, 64, *65*
    Grilled Tri-Tip Roast, 62
    Perfect Prime Rib, 63
    Picante Pot Roast, 62
    Sizzlin' Southwest Steak, 66
Berry Almond Cream Trifle, 95
Big Apple Martini, 100
Black Bean Basil Salsa, 10
Bread Pudding, 85
Breakfast
    Chile con Huevos, 39
    Crème Brûlée Pancakes, 40, *41*

Fiesta Breakfast, 38, *38*
Pumpkin Pancakes, 42
Southwest Sunday Quiche, 39
Bruschette, *16*, 17
Bumble Bee, 104

Cactus Colada Martini, 102
Caesar Salad, 29
Cake, Yellow Ribbon, 91
Champagne Bar, 105
Cheese
    Baked Artichoke Queso, 19
    Pastrami and Pepper Jack Wraps, 49, *49*
    Pepper Garlic Cheese Bread, 18
    Sweet Hot Cheese Spread, 19
Cheese butters
    Garlic Basil, 80
    Jalapeño Jack, 80
Cheesecake Cream, 14
Cherry La Bombas, 88, *89*
Chicken
    Chicken Piccata Olé, 52
    Chipotle Chicken Pizza, 45
    Crusted Pecan Chicken, 51
    Garlic Chicken on Sourdough, 43
    Grilled Garlic Chicken, 54, *55*
    Margarita Chicken, 50
    Sopa de Lima, 24, *25*
    Sopa de Pollo, 23
    Sour Cream Chicken Enchiladas, 50
    Spicy Chicken Stir Fry, 52
Chiles
    Chile con Huevos, 39
    Chile Corn Chowder, 26, 27
    Chile Mashed Potatoes, 77
    Chile Shrimp Caliente, 70, *71*
    Chile-Spiced Pecans, 11
    Chipotle Chicken Pizza, 45
    Chipotle Ranch Dressing, 67
    Green Chile Enchiladas, 53
    Green Chile Relleno Bake, 76
    Green Chile Turkey Stew, 22
    Honey Glazed Ham with Green Chile
        Relish, 60
    Jalapeño Glazed Halibut, 70
Chipotle Chicken Pizza, 45
Chipotle Ranch Dressing, 67
Chocolate
    Cherry La Bombas, 88, *89*
    Decadent Dippers, 86, *87*
    Mexican Chocolate Drizzle Sauce, 91

Chowders
    Baked Potato Chowder, 27, 28
    Chile Corn Chowder, 26, 27
    Spicy Sun Bowl Chowder, 22
Cocktails
    Big Apple Martini, 100
    Bumble Bee, 104
    Cactus Colada Martini, 102
    Champagne Bar, 105
    Electric Pink Lemonade, 105
    Margarita Classico, 104
    Mexican Madras Martini, 102
    Michilada, 98
    Pink Cadillac Margarita, 100, *101*
    Prioska, 99
    Sangria Spritzer, 99
    Sunny Champagne Punch, 103
    Sunshine Breakfast Cocktail, 103
Corn, Fresh Roasted, 78, *79*
Crème Brûlée Pancakes, 40, *41*
Crusted Baked Squash, 76
Crusted Pecan Chicken, 51

Decadent Dippers, 86, *87*
Desserts
    Bananas Olé, 94
    Berry Almond Cream Trifle, 95
    Cherry La Bombas, 88, *89*
    Decadent Dippers, 86, *87*
    Fresh Mango Martinis, 90
    Margarita Pie, 92, *93*
    Mexican Bread Pudding, 85
    Pecan Pie, 84
    Praline Peach Cobbler, 84
    Strawberries and Mexican Chocolate
        Drizzle Sauce, 91
    Sweet Tortilla Cups, 94
    Watermelon Sorbet, 95
    Yellow Ribbon Cake, 91
Dips. *See also* Decadent Dippers, Sauces
    Amaretto Cream, 14
    Cheesecake Cream, 14
Dressings
    Chipotle Ranch Dressing, 67
    Lemon Vinaigrette, 32
    Lite Caesar Dressing, 29
Drinks. *See* Cocktails

Eggs
    Chile con Huevos, 39
    Fiesta Breakfast, 38, *38*
Electric Pink Lemonade, 105

Enchiladas
    Green Chile Enchiladas, 53
    Sour Cream Chicken Enchiladas, 50
Entrées
    Baja Tacos with Chipotle Ranch
        Dressing, 67
    Chicken Piccata Olé, 52
    Chile Shrimp Caliente, 70, 71
    Crusted Pecan Chicken, 51
    Garlic Rosemary Pork Tenderloin, 61
    Gingered Beef Short Ribs, 63
    Green Chile Enchiladas, 53
    Grilled Garlic Chicken, 54, 55
    Grilled Rib-Eye Steak with Jalapeño
        Salsa, 64, 65
    Grilled Ribs with Apple Bourbon
        Sauce, 58, 59
    Grilled Tri-Tip Roast, 62
    Honey Glazed Ham with Green Chile
        Relish, 60
    Jalapeño Glazed Halibut, 70
    Lobster Marinara and Pasta Amor, 68, 69
    Margarita Chicken, 50
    Marinated Pork Loin Chops, 56, 57
    Perfect Prime Rib, 63
    Picante Pot Roast, 62
    Pork Loin Fajitas, 60
    Sizzlin' Southwest Steak, 66
    Sour Cream Chicken Enchiladas, 50
    Spicy Chicken Stir Fry, 52

Fall dishes, 107
Festive Caesar Salad, 29
Fiesta Breakfast, 38, 38
Fish and seafood
    Baja Tacos with Chipotle Ranch
        Dressing, 67
    Chile Shrimp Caliente, 70, 71
    Jalapeño Glazed Halibut, 70
    Lobster Marinara and Pasta Amor, 68, 69
Focaccia, 18
Fresh Basil-Tomato Summer Salad, 32, 35
Fresh Fruit and Sweet Creams, 14
Fresh ingredients, 1
Fresh Mango Martinis, 90
Fresh Roasted Corn with Butter Herb Sauce, 59,
    78, 79
Fresh Salsa Verde, 8
Fruit
    Apple-Onion-Garlic Salsa, 9
    Bananas Olé, 94
    Berry Almond Cream Trifle, 95

Cherry La Bombas, 88, 89
Decadent Dippers, 86, 87
Fresh Fruit and Sweet Creams, 14
Fresh Mango Martinis, 90
Raspberry Drizzle Sauce, 90
Sopa de Lima, 24, 25
Strawberries and Mexican Chocolate
    Drizzle Sauce, 91
Strawberry and Spinach Holiday Salad,
    34, 35
Watermelon Sorbet, 95

Garden Quesadilla, 43
Garden Salsa Nachos, 15
Garlic Basil Butter, 80
Garlic Chicken on Sourdough, 43
Garlic Oil, 45
Garlic Rosemary Pork Tenderloin, 61
Gingered Beef Short Ribs, 63
Green beans, 30, 31
Green Chile Enchiladas, 53
Green Chile Relleno Bake, 76
Green Chile Turkey Stew, 22
Grilled Garlic Chicken, 54, 55
Grilled Rib-Eye Steak with Jalapeño Salsa, 64, 65
Grilled Ribs with Apple Bourbon Sauce, 58, 59
Grilled Tri-Tip Roast, 62

Ham, Honey Glazed, 60
Homemade Pizza Crust, 45
Honey Glazed Ham with Green Chile Relish, 60
Huevos rancheros. See Fiesta Breakfast

Jalapeño Glazed Halibut, 70
Jalapeño Jack Butter, 80

"Kelly's Kitchen," 1–2

Latino Salsa Salad, 29, 31
Lemon Vinaigrette, 32
Libations. See Cocktails
Light bites
    Chipotle Chicken Pizza, 45
    Garden Quesadilla, 43
    Garlic Chicken on Sourdough, 43
    Garlic Oil, 45
    Homemade Pizza Crust, 45
    Pastrami and Pepper Jack Wraps, 49, 49
    Pesto Artichoke Pizza, 44
    Red Pepper Tostadas, 46, 47
    Turkey, Avocado, and Pepper Wraps,
        48, 48

Lite Caesar Dressing, 29
Lobster Marinara and Pasta Amor, 68, 69

Main meals. See Breakfast, Entrées, Light bites
Mango Salsa, 10
Margarita Chicken, 50
Margarita Classico, 104
Margarita Pie, 92, 93
Marinated Pork Loin Chops, 56, 57
Mexican Bread Pudding, 85
Mexican Chocolate Drizzle Sauce, 91
Mexican Madras Martini, 102
Michilada, 98
Mushrooms
    Spicy Stuffed Mushrooms, 12, 13
    Verde Fresco Salad, 30, 31

Nachos
    Garden Salsa, 15
    Rancheros, 15
Nuts
    Berry Almond Cream Trifle, 95
    Chile-Spiced Pecans, 11
    Crusted Pecan Chicken, 51
    Pecan Pie, 84
    Praline Peach Cobbler, 84

Pancakes
    Crème Brûlée, 40, 41
    Pumpkin, 42
Pastrami and Pepper Jack Wraps, 49, 49
Pecan Pie, 84
Pepper Garlic Cheese Bread, 18
Perfect Prime Rib, 63
Pesto Tomato Bruschette, 16, 17
Pesto Artichoke Pizza, 44
Picante Pot Roast, 62
Pico de Gallo, 8
Pies
    Margarita, 92, 93
    Pecan, 84
Pink Cadillac Margarita, 100, 101
Pinto Beans and Chile, 23
Pizza
    Chipotle Chicken Pizza, 45
    Homemade Crust, 45
    Pesto Artichoke Pizza, 44
Pork
    Garlic Rosemary Pork Tenderloin, 61
    Grilled Ribs with Apple Bourbon
        Sauce, 58, 59

Honey Glazed Ham with Green Chile
  Relish, 60
Marinated Pork Loin Chops, 56, *57*
Pork Loin Fajitas, 60
Potatoes
  Baby Red Potato Salad, 33
  Baked Potato Buffet with Cheese
    Butters, 80
  Baked Potato Chowder, 27, 28
  Chile Mashed Potatoes, 77
  Red Chile Spuds, 81
Praline Peach Cobbler, 84
Prioska, 99
Pumpkin Pancakes, 42

Quesadillas, 43
Quiche, 39

Raspberry Drizzle Sauce, 90
Red Chile Spuds, 81
Red Pepper Tostadas, 46, *47*
Rice
  Arroz Verde, 74
  Spanish Rice, 74
Roasted Vegetables, 77
Rosemary Garlic Focaccia Bread, 18

Salads
  Baby Red Potato Salad, 33
  Festive Caesar Salad, 29
  Fresh Basil-Tomato Summer Salad,
    32, *35*
  Latino Salsa Salad, 29, *31*
  Southwest Bacon, Lettuce, and
    Tomato Salad, 33
  Spicy Winter Greens, 32
  Strawberry and Spinach Holiday Salad,
    34, *35*
  Verde Fresco Salad, 30, *31*
Salsa
  Apple-Onion-Garlic Salsa, 9
  Black Bean Basil Salsa, 10
  Fresh Salsa Verde, 8
  Latino Salsa Salad, 29, *31*
  Mango Salsa, 10
  Pico de Gallo, 8
  Sassy Shrimp Salsa, 11
  Zucchini Salsa Bake, 75
Sangria Spritzer, 99
Sassy Shrimp Salsa, 11
Sauces. *See also* Dips, Dressings
  Asian Dipping Sauce, 51

Mexican Chocolate Drizzle Sauce, 91
Raspberry Drizzle Sauce, 90
Vanilla Cream Sauce, 85
Seafood. *See* Fish and seafood
Seasonal approach, 2
Seasonal selections, 106–107
7/30 cooking concept, 1
Shrimp. *See* Fish and seafood
  Sassy Shrimp Salsa, 11
  Spicy Sun Bowl Chowder, 22
Side dishes
  Arroz Verde, 74
  Baked Potato Buffet with Cheese
    Butters, 80
  Chile Mashed Potatoes, 77
  Crusted Baked Squash, 76
  Fresh Roasted Corn with Butter Herb
    Sauce, *59*, 78, *79*
  Garlic Basil Butter, 80
  Green Chile Relleno Bake, 76
  Jalapeño Jack Butter, 80
  Red Chile Spuds, 81
  Roasted Vegetables, 77
  Spanish Rice, 74
  Sun-Grilled Veggies, *65*, 75
  Zucchini Salsa Bake, 75
Sizzlin' Southwest Steak, 66
Snacks. *See also* Light bites
  Chile-Spiced Pecans, 11
  Southwest Snack Mix, 6, *7*
Sopa de Lima, 24, *25*
Sopa de Pollo, 23
Soups
  Baked Potato Chowder, 27, 28
  Chile Corn Chowder, 26, *27*
  Green Chile Turkey Stew, 22
  Pinto Beans and Chile, 23
  Sopa de Lima, 24, *25*
  Sopa de Pollo, 23
  Spicy Sun Bowl Chowder, 22
Sour Cream Chicken Enchiladas, 50
Southwest Bacon, Lettuce, and Tomato Salad, 33
Southwest Snack Mix, 6, *7*
Southwest Sunday Quiche, 39
Southwestern cuisine, 1, 2
Spanish Rice, 74
Spicy Chicken Stir Fry, 52
Spicy Stuffed Mushrooms, 12, *13*
Spicy Sun Bowl Chowder, 22
Spicy Winter Greens, 32
Spring dishes, 106
Starters. *See* Appetizers, Salsas, Snacks

Strawberries and Mexican Chocolate Drizzle
  Sauce, 91
Strawberry and Spinach Holiday Salad, 34, *35*
Summer dishes, 106
Sun-Grilled Veggies, *65*, 75
Sunny Champagne Punch, 103
Sunshine Breakfast Cocktail, 103
Sweet Hot Cheese Spread, 19
Sweet Tortilla Cups, 94
Sweets. *See* Desserts

Tacos, 67
Time-saving tips, 3
Tomatoes
  Fresh Basil-Tomato Summer Salad,
    32, *35*
  Southwest Bacon, Lettuce, and
    Tomato Salad, 33
Tortilla Cups, 94
Tostadas, 46, *47*
Turkey
  Turkey, Avocado, and Pepper Wraps,
    48, *48*
  Green Chile Turkey Stew, 22

Vanilla Cream Sauce, 85
Vegetables. *See also* Chiles, Potatoes, Salads, Salsas
  Crusted Baked Squash, 76
  Fresh Roasted Corn with Butter Herb
    Sauce, *59*, 78, *79*
  Roasted Vegetables, 77
  Sun-Grilled Veggies, *65*, 75
  Zucchini Salsa Bake, 75
Verde Fresco Salad, 30, *31*

Watermelon Sorbet, 95
Winter dishes, 107
Wraps
  Pastrami and Pepper Jack Wraps, 49, *49*
  Turkey, Avocado, and Pepper Wraps,
    48, *48*

Yellow Ribbon Cake, 91

Zucchini Salsa Bake, 75

MANY, MANY THANKS to all my viewers and fans of "Kelley's Kitchen." Allow me to applaud you. Your comments, recipes, and friendship over the last 5 years have made me a better cook and my job at KTSM a complete joy. I want to thank Larry Bracher, Eric Pearson, and Richard Pearson for their unconditional support of "Kelley's Kitchen." A special hug goes to Dennis Quintana of KTSM for his technical expertise, emotional support, and many laughs. It has been a blast! And many thanks go to the morning crew at News Channel 9 in El Paso for believing in me and allowing me to share my "7-ingredient/30 minute" recipes with the viewers of West Texas and southern New Mexico every week since 1998. I love you all!

Again, my most sincere and heartfelt "thank you" goes to two people who made this book a reality. First, my Agent, Lisa Ekus, who understands my desire to write and cook for others. Thank you for guiding me through this writing experience; and second, to Ken Bookman for his incredible ability to make everything sound better and for keeping me focused and on schedule. It has been a pleasure.

To my Publisher, Dave Jenney, and my Editor, Tammy Gales, thank you for the opportunity to write *Simply 7*. It has been a wonderful experience. I would also like to thank my book designer, Katie Jennings, and my food stylists, Judy Reynolds and Ellen Straine, for their creative talents. And of course, a very special thank you to Christopher Marchetti and his assistant Lindy Terrell for their incredible photography.

This book could not have been written without the help of so many wonderful people. To the entire Cleary family, thank you for always being there for my children and me. To Bob and Linda Skolnick and my friends at Mountain Dreams Publishing, thank you for your support and allowing me do my thing! A special thank you goes to Lori Buhl and Holly Cleary for entertaining my two darlings. To my two darlings, Daniel and Brooke, thanks for grocery shopping and hanging out in the kitchen with me. You make it fun. Much gratitude also goes to the staff at Albertsons, my local grocery store. Your friendly faces and great service make my constant shopping experiences enjoyable. Finally, a huge thank you to all my girlfriends and neighbors for watching my kids, sampling my food, and giving me your honest opinions.

KELLEY CLEARY COFFEEN was born and raised in the Southwest. She is the author of *Fiesta Mexicali* by Northland Publishing and the *Great College Cookbook of the Southwest,* which was featured on "Good Morning America." As a home economist, Kelley enjoys sharing timesaving tips and lifestyle management ideas on her popular weekly television show "Kelley's Kitchen." Kelley also handles product development and customer relations for a regional publishing company. She lives in Las Cruces, New Mexico with her family.